MUSEUM
COLLECTION
ETHICS

MUSEUM COLLECTION ETHICS

ACQUISITION, STEWARDSHIP, AND INTERPRETATION

STEVEN MILLER

ROWMAN & LITTLEFIELD
Lanham • Boulder • New York • London

Published by Rowman & Littlefield
An imprint of The Rowman & Littlefield Publishing Group, Inc.
4501 Forbes Boulevard, Suite 200, Lanham, Maryland 20706
www.rowman.com

6 Tinworth Street, London SE11 5AL, United Kingdom

British Library Cataloguing in Publication Information Available

Library of Congress Cataloging-in-Publication Data Available

ISBN 978-1-5381-3519-8 (cloth : alk. paper)
ISBN 978-1-5381-3520-4 (pbk. : alk. paper)
ISBN 978-1-5381-3521-1 (electronic)

∞™ The paper used in this publication meets the minimum requirements of American National Standard for Information Sciences—Permanence of Paper for Printed Library Materials, ANSI/NISO Z39.48-1992.

To my late parents,
Ann Stevens Miller and Charles C. Miller.
My mother was an early childhood educator
and my father an interior designer
and decorated World War II veteran.
Everyone enjoyed their natural sense of ethics.

CONTENTS

LIST OF ILLUSTRATIONS

PREFACE

Ethics are the operational principals or value systems that govern an individual's or group's behavior. Unlike the law, which has an enforcement mechanism built in through the legal system, ethics are largely unenforceable except through the self-policing by the individual group who adopts the particular ethical code.[1]

At times it can be easy to confuse ethics and the law, as they often overlap both in topics covered and application. However, they are not the same, and the distinction should be remembered whenever a discussion involving either ethics or the law is undertaken.[2]

The subject of museum ethics has been of major public interest since the 1960s. During that tumultuous decade of political, economic, demographic, and cultural upheaval, especially in the United States, museums were the target of behavior complaints. These assaults largely focused on how relevant or irrelevant museums were for society at large and specific groups. Arguments were made that museums had to act in a more overtly ethical manner to justify their existence, especially as tax-exempt public entities. Controversies centered on who "owned" museums and what perspectives were provided in galleries. Were museums for the privileged few or the ordinary person? How diverse were museums insofar as audiences, employees, and content were concerned?

In the decades following the 1960s, the ways in which museums did their work became a popular topic. It is now front and center as a museum subject. And, regardless of the conversation, institutional behavior is always referenced. When people express opinions on museum exhibitions, acquisitions, programming, architecture, finances, or a personnel issue, ethics is often part of the discussion. Workshops, articles, essays, talks, and a host of internet exchanges ceaselessly engage the topic. This has been all to the good. Anyone in the museum profession for a long time knows the absent way ethical considerations were once handled. Today, the subject is a central concern of the field. Individual museums have self-generated codes of ethics as do museum professional membership organizations.

When it comes to ethics, what museums address most are matters of personnel, mission inclusion or exclusion, and certain aspects of collection acquisition, retention, and interpretation. These topics are discussed in several relevant publications but always as an inclusive group. While overarching conversations about museum activities are valued, collection issues as a unique subject remains to be addressed. No single publication covers museum collection ethics in any comprehensive manner. This book is designed to fill that gap.

Collections define museums. Indeed—no collection, no museum! Consequently, nothing museums do involves ethical considerations more than the intellectual construct and practices regarding what they own for public benefit. "The distinctive character of museum ethics derives from the ownership, care and use of objects, specimens, and living collections representing the world's natural and cultural common wealth."[3] How these things are obtained, kept, cared for, used, accessed, and on occasion disposed of, all have ethics ramifications. *Museum Collection Ethics* attempts to outline a full range of moral and behavioral duties that museums owe to maintaining and preserving their collections, such as not breaking objects, failing to catalog them, exposing them to poor handling, etc.

With nearly fifty years' working experience in the field as a curator, director, trustee, educator, writer, consultant, and critic, I have dealt with museum collections from every perspective imaginable. Cumulatively, I have acquired thousands of objects for the six museums I have worked in since 1971. I have been responsible for assuring the cataloging, researching, publishing, storing, reproducing, conserving, exhibiting, bringing to media attention, and even deaccessioning of a great variety of objects. Ethical concerns apply in all these duties. What they are, how they are determined, and who is responsible for them in whatever form they take depends on many factors. There is no "one size fits all" approach to museum collection ethics. Circumstances vary. Nuances reign. Opinions differ. This book is not an outsider's perspective. It is an insider's explanation of museum collections as they reflect and embrace ethics realities today. While I attempt to discuss collection ethics from as many perspectives as possible (again based on my experience, augmented by that of colleagues and what I read in the museum and mainstream press these days), my writing is not comprehensive. Moreover, I am sure I have either neglected aspects of importance or given them short shrift. I apologize for these failures, but I hope I have started a focused conversation that will permeate the field to the advantage of museum collections and those responsible for them.

I have enormous respect for those in the museum profession who devote their work-a-day lives to the hands-on and intellectual well-being of the material evidence held in public trust in museums of all sizes. These positions largely include collection managers, curators, registrars, and conservators (appendix I). Some directors meet the profile, also, but these days those jobs are almost totally devoted to administration and fundraising. Boards of trustees, who are the self-appointed legal overseers of museums, are usually immaterial participants when it comes to collection realities. Unfortunately they can cause the most damage. Fortunately they do not. I cite a few examples of trustee transgressions I have encountered regarding museum collection ethics. These simply illustrate important points I wish to make. There is nothing like personal experience to inform reality. Therefore, my narratives are infused with on-the-job situations that might be of interest to readers and make a point in ways a more general comment would not. Museum workers are practical people. Facts are more effective when it comes to communicating than idealized generic mumbo jumbo.

Organization

The first chapter discusses defining a museum. This is essential to agree to and accept when addressing collection matters. On the surface, it may seem a rudimentary and even simplistic exercise, but in fact it must be examined considering today's museological practices and operating wishes. It must also be explained that the word "museum" need not be in an institution's name though it meets the definition of such a place. Museums can legitimately be called galleries, collections, societies, centers, and foundations.

Once the definition of museums is agreed upon, there must be a discussion of how they legally exist and who is responsible for their oversight. Chapter 2 addresses this subject. It establishes ethics discussions as a consideration anticipating how the topic must infuse everything museums do insofar as their unique character is concerned—getting, owning, and caring for objects of cultural value. The following chapter delves into the breadth of ethical considerations that relate to everything museums do with what items they seek, keep, and dispose of. Who has legal authority over museum collections is explained in terms of ethical behaviors in chapter 4. Because how museums collect is so critical to current or subsequent ethical questions, acquisition initiatives, processes, and outcomes are the interconnected themes of chapter 5. Few people know about the intricacies of museum collecting yet it is this activity that must be pursued with the utmost veracity and transparency. Chapter 6 drills into the topic with an emphasis on behaviors related to museum collecting.

Once collections have been formed, museums have a wide range of ethical concerns they must be aware of and attend to while at the same time being attuned to unanticipated ones. The scope of positive and negative entanglements can be alarming. Museums are targets of a variety of assaults about moral, or immoral, behaviors. Sometimes these are justified but often they are matters of cultural or individual opinions.

Chapter 7 discusses the critical subject of collection authenticity. Are the things museums have, use, and preserve what they say they are? What should museums do if they discover fakes in their collections? Having collections must require taking proper care of them and making them available for safe use. While there have long been accepted and unaccepted ways to store, document, and provide access to collections, there are new ethics regarding these measures. Chapter 8 delves into this evolving subject. The conservation of museum collections has shifted from a craft to a science. The reasons for and ramifications of physical actions on collections must be understood in a much broader way than was once the case. Chapter 9 offers information on this increasingly complex realm of collection ethics. Finally, the most common way museum publics encounter original museum collections is through exhibitions. Chapter 10 reviews ethics regarding what is shown, how, and why. The impact of outside forces on exhibit themes, content, and presentations will only grow. Museums must be ever-vigilant for new influences in this regard. Chapter 11 discusses the ethics of museum collection losses, both deliberate and accidental. The very idea of museums removing or losing their collections can be disturbing at best and catastrophic at worse. These feelings are largely voiced by outsiders to the museum field, but murmured agreements are certainly heard within the profession itself.

The final chapter suggests that museums establish collection ethics standards. While some of the guidelines would be contained in collection policies, the scope and intent are broader and include governing bodies, the institution itself, and staff and volunteers. The last group is not often acknowledged when it comes to how museum collections are acquired, maintained, and used, but given the role volunteers play in all these areas, increased attention must include them in all the field's mission and operating applications.

The Ethics in Action scenarios presented at the end of each chapter are drawn from real-life situations. I have encountered many of them. Colleagues have experienced and graciously contributed others. A few are drawn from the media as they clearly involve collection ethics conundrums. The Ethics in Action lists are offered for discussion purposes. Responses to some may be clear but murky for others. When this book is used in a museum studies context, participants are urged to add examples for discussion purposes. While a "one-size-fits-all" approach to museum ethics is difficult to apply across the board, there are many overlapping debates to be aware of.

The appendices are included to show ways museums and museum-related organizations formally address ethics of institutional and professional concern. While an entire book could be devoted to examples and still be incomplete, these examples refer to aspects of this volume's information. Each is well constructed to meet the current needs and objects for their application. Anyone wishing to pursue further information is invited to contact the institutions and organizations referenced.

There are several books devoted to museum ethics or referencing the subject in a helpful capacity. Current editions of note are listed in the short bibliography. They offer overarching considerations of the topic and are well worth reading. More will be written. Museum professionals are encouraged to be mindful of future ethics issues and how they will be discussed in print (in hard copy or cyberspace), in the spoken word, or in whatever verbal vehicle provided in conferences, online, etc. The media at large must always be monitored for unfolding museum collection news. Indeed, it is often the first place new or renewed collection issues emerge.

Museum Collection Ethics is the first publication to dwell exclusively on dominant ethics issues boiling within the museum world. The subject is complex. It will only become more so as those within the profession refine collection acquisition, stewardship, and interpretation. Forces beyond museums will perhaps have the most impact, though. We have already seen the effects of outside influences in causing museums to change, or at least rethink, what they collect, why, how, and what they do with long-held possessions. It is the goal of this book to introduce the range of concerns that all museums must accept as they continue to be unique public institutions of value.

Notes

1. Heather Hope Kuruvilla, *A Legal Dictionary for Museum Professionals* (Lanham, MD: Rowman & Littlefield, 2016), 69.
2. Ibid., 171.
3. Sally Yerkovich, *A Practical Guide to Museum Ethics* (Lanham, MD: Rowman & Littlefield, 2016), 4.

ACKNOWLEDGMENTS

The substance of this book reflects the wonderful editing prowess of Sandy Wood. Without her expertise the results of my efforts would be weak at best. She has unerringly guided my writing and corrected my lapses. This is her third book keeping me on the right writing track. I am thankful!

Discussing ethics can go on forever. Insofar as they involve museum collections, the topic can be somewhat controlled, but there is still a lot of room for interpretation. During my career, I have been fortunate to learn from wise mentors. These included the late Joe Noble, director of the Museum of the City of New York, and the late Barry Baragwanath, senior curator of that institution. Paul Rivard, director of the Maine State Museum was an exemplary (not to mention hilarious) model of ethical behavior.

For this book, individuals who helped me assemble model codes of ethics and related documents for the appendices include: Cecelia Wells, content and editorial Strategist for the American Alliance of Museums, facilitated the inclusion of its Curators Committee Code of Ethics; Bonnie Naugle, communications and membership director of the American Institute of Conservation, helped make possible the use of its conservators code of ethics; the Open Access press could be used thanks to Caroline Guscott, director of communications and external relations;

Julianna Whalen confirmed my use of the University of Pennsylvania museum's Statement on Human Remains.

Finally, my wife Jane is the epitome of an ethical person and has even been cited for such by her long-time employer, the Nature Conservancy. It is a treat to be married to such a model leader in the nonprofit sector.

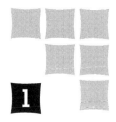

DEFINING A MUSEUM

A museum is a non-profit, permanent institution in the service of society and its development, open to the public, which acquires, conserves, researches, communicates and exhibits the tangible and intangible heritage of humanity and its environment for the purposes of education, study and enjoyment.[1]

What's a museum? And, what does a definition have to do with museum collection ethics? The definition of a museum (above) from the International Council of Museums (ICOM) is in the process of being discussed by its members. As of this writing, while settling on a new definition about who museums serve and why will be subject to debate, their core object-centric character will remain what defines and makes them unique. Understanding this is central to establishing why they exist and how they operate. This chapter discusses how a museum's definition of itself influences every aspect of its ethical concerns.

The Object of a Museum

Individual museum profiles are referenced in mission statements and associated documents. Internal scholarship, media output, and public programming support a commonly agreed-upon identity. Given the altruistic idea of a museum, few museums exist to do ill, regardless of what some might think of their work.

Museums are peculiar operations. They make no practical sense whatsoever. Why are there places dedicated to collecting all sorts of objects with the idea of retaining them in perpetuity for some alleged public good? The world got along fine without museums for millennia. To be sure, art, artifacts, and scientific specimens have been venerated, studied, and enjoyed for whatever reasons since humans left evidence of such interests. But the idea of focusing on subjects to be explored and explained through relevant materials collected in a disciplined manner and for a long time is unusual to say the least.

Who decided to create non-income-producing storehouses of the tangible acquired to serve intangible interests? The conceptual and actual history of the museum as we know it is fascinating and clear. They are Western inventions that grew out of the Enlightenment and the age of exploration. Scholars, explorers, politicians, and cultural entrepreneurs found objects to be of immense personal and didactic value. That work initially focused on examining and explaining the human and natural universe to and for a broad base of professional as well as amateur academics. In time, rather quickly on occasion, making the results of the work available to a public became a meaningful purpose. The inception of the museum and its early evolution set the tone for these operations almost from their start. They have remained essentially unchanged since their creation.

The ethics of museums flow from their unusual defined character. Understanding and accepting that character is essential to how all associated with the field behave. Museums evolved from two precedents. One took the form of private collections of art, artifacts, and natural history curiosities. The other contained the same sorts of things but was assembled and shown in a formal capacity as propaganda to support established religions or political powers. In eighteenth-century Europe, new intellectual interests emerged that caused objects to be seen for intrinsic rather than extrinsic meanings. To be sure, depending on the institution and its operators, what is seen in museums can still play their previous roles or variants thereof, but those applications have largely dissolved or been shunted aside for more mainstream informational applications. Thus, a fifteenth-century painting of the crucifixion of Jesus Christ shown in an art museum is presented in an art historical mode rather than for purposes of worship.

The only thing that separates museums from other human endeavors is having permanent, physical collections for the general good. No other entities in any society do this. For practical reasons museums easily can be considered public service preservation organizations that explain subjects through objects, and the objects are original evidence of the subjects being examined. This working definition is easily parsed.

Defining Museums as Public Service

Public service means being of civic benefit for altruistic reasons. This role of a museum is declared in founding documents, organizational records, and mission statements. It is extolled regularly in exhibitions, educational programs, publications, media materials, acquisition announcements, etc. The public service museums provide was rarely forced on them by disinterested outsiders or government authorities. For the most part, it is entirely voluntary and self-generated.

Museums as we know them today were and continue to be founded by individuals with an interest in a subject they feel can best be promoted through relevant art, historic artifacts, and scientific specimens that are original to a topic. In this capacity they are celebratory in nature. Being of service to the general populace or a portion thereof requires transparency in just about all aspects of the work done by an institution. This sets an ethical principle.

In the United States the philanthropic nature of museums puts most in the governing legal category of a private nonprofit charity. This allows them to be tax exempt, which brings various operating benefits. They are exempt from real estate taxes. They need not pay tax on purchases. And, donations to them qualify for tax deductions by the donor if he or she meets Internal Revenue Service guidelines. It also acknowledges the public character of their purpose. This distinction is of extreme importance, especially when it comes to ethics. Museums must set and abide by a higher level of trust and behavior than might be the case with businesses.

Museums are not commercial ventures, though they may dabble in profit-making activities. But there are some entities that appear to be museums yet are not. These have museum-type collections, engage in museum-type activities, and practice museum profession procedures.

From a collection perspective, what they own and present to people is often highly attractive, historic, and culturally valuable. Three examples of corporations that have museum component operations are the Wells Fargo financial company; Ripley's Believe It or Not; and the Hard Rock corporation. All three have great collections of artifacts reflecting the history of their businesses. These things are on view in their various business locations around the globe.

When it comes to their collection base, what sets these companies' holdings apart from museums is the fact that the objects are business assets which can be, and often are, subject to retention, alteration, or sale simply for commercial reasons. The objects are not kept for high-minded informational, spiritual, or cultural preservation reasons. This absolves corporate collections from many of the ethical concerns that museums have regarding collections. What a business acquires is not gotten or kept as museum collections are. The things we see in a museum-like corporate environment play financial roles. This difference is hardly a criticism of company collections. Corporations, like individuals, may (legally we hope) do as they wish with the material goods of the human and natural world.

A growing public service aspect of museum operations today flows from the idea of the museum-as-attraction. For at least two centuries, most museums have been able to welcome visitors in some regularly scheduled manner. For years they have been listed in tourist brochures and promoted by travel bureaus. They developed membership programs that encouraged visitation. Any city boasting a cultural site open to the public hardly kept it a secret. Now, however, the crushing need for more and more operating money has set museums on an intense track to get more and more visitors. The ethics of this reality has an impact on collections. Do museums only collect things that will attract visitors? Should they get rid of objects that are not carrying their exhibition weight—meaning they stay in storage or are retained only for esoteric scholarly research purposes rather than luring in customers? Is a robust program of changing and special exhibits necessary to increase attendance revenue? If so, does this priority deflect attention and resources from more mission-centric but hidden work?

Museums themselves are largely responsible for the museum-as-attraction phenomenon. It erupted with a vengeance in the 1960s with the creation of what became known as the blockbuster exhibition. These extravagant productions are historically credited to New York City's Metropolitan Museum of Art and Washington, DC's National Gallery of Art. The respective director protagonists were Thomas P. F. Hoving and J. Carter Brown. Though these two institutions and men set a crushing pace, scores of other museums were participants. Soon visitation was the easiest way to judge a museum's apparent success. Attendance statistics became markers of relevance and accomplishment. Boards of trustees who were (and remain) largely comprised of businessmen found these numbers an easy way to measure "their" museum's effectiveness.

For some, the ardent focus on the gate had, and continues to have, an adverse museum ethics impact. A previous emphasis on retaining and improving the quality, scope, and informational value of collections is of less merit insofar as boards of trustees are concerned. Entertainment (euphemistically referred to as audience engagement) has supplanted scholarship. While the content verbiage found in exhibitions reeks of learning, the naming of exhibits and how they are "sold" to the general public is pure hucksterism. Certainly, traditional forms of museum fundraising continue, including quests for philanthropic support, corporate underwriting, and government largess. But as museums have grown and become more expensive to run, they are expanding their ability to earn income along the lines of commercial tourist destinations. Do attendance factors have ethic ramifications? Yes. Are these ramifications positive, negative, or negligible? Yes. Maybe. No.

Most people do not visit museums. Individuals have many things to occupy their free time outside the home or places of employment. This visitation absence hardly suggests museums are disliked. On the contrary, they are often admired and appreciated, if only at a distance or when asked by a museum attendance pollster. I can offer a personal analogy. I have never been to a professional football game and have no interest in ever doing so. Indeed, I rarely watch the sport (or any sports) on television. This does not mean I dislike football. I just have other things I prefer to do.

Studying museum visitation realities is an all-consuming and important task these days. From small, volunteer organizations to large, wealthy institutions, museum boards of trustees and administrators increasingly attempt to know why people go to a museum and why they do not. It is virtually impossible to discover the latter but easy to ascertain the former. The quality of such surveys varies. If well done, the results will inform how museums define themselves, at least for operational purposes. The learning will suggest how ethics, among other considerations, will be embraced going forward. If a museum learns that something it does is ethically questioned by visitors, then that activity should cease or be reconstructed. Historic southern American plantations are discovering this when they fail to acknowledge the central place of slavery in their histories. They are beginning to redefine themselves insofar as this part of their heritage is concerned.

Defining the Museum Preservation Imperative

The word "preservation" in our practical characterization of museums embraces collections and subjects. Museums save what they collect in the service of saving the subject for which they exist. Ultimately, objects have two destinies: They can disappear forever, or they can find their way into museums. Accepting this notion means the acquisition act is a form of preservation. The ethics of deciding what is to be saved and what is to be rejected will ebb and flow over time.

In application, preserving collections is a ceaseless duty involving a range of passive and active measures. Passive measures include providing static safe storage, timely and accurate record keeping, and a sustainable commitment to future institutional continuity. Active preservation measures primarily involve conservation physically done to objects and monitoring protective housing circumstance and conditions for individual items.

Defining the Museum as Organization

Museums must be organized in some structural governing and administrative manner. Few museums survive if they do not exist in a legal as well as actual form. Being an organization means being a human undertaking involving individuals who work (for free or pay) to make something happen and sustain that devotion. In the case of museums, it also means there is a physical manifestation of the organization. It is unethical to attempt to have a museum while failing to be a viable organization.

The idea of a virtual museum may be intellectually intriguing but like having a virtual home, there is no there, there.

Defining Museums as Places of Explanation

The museum charge to explain is applied in several ways. Most notably it is seen in the communication forum of the exhibition, but it also is done in hard copy and through online verbal/visual information mechanisms. The process of collecting is an explanation exercise itself as museum employees decide how to help with present and future teaching needs. Ethics concerns in this process unfold on a case-by-case basis.

Defining Museum Subjects

Museums self-select the subjects they choose to be about. The variety is astonishing. New museums are founded constantly. Deciding on what subjects to celebrate has ethical implications that can range from great to negligible. Collections will be the center of initial and subsequent discussions. This was certainly the case for the National Museum of African American History and Culture on the mall in Washington, DC. When conceived, it had no collections. Now it does and they are terrific. Everything is direct evidence of the African American experience in this country.

Defining Original Objects in Museums

Because objects are at the core of a museum's being, how original they are to an institution's subject is critical to collection acquisition and retention. As previously noted, objects play the role of evidence. In that capacity, the most effective and meaningful pieces are directly relevant to the topic being preserved by a museum. Original and relevant means an item was made, used, or otherwise involved with aspects of a museum's historic, artistic, or scientific purpose.

Defining a Museum's Ethics

Museum ethics will include interpersonal relations, corporate legal matters, employment concerns, and operational behaviors. These are shared by all sorts of for-profit and nonprofit work environments.

What is exclusive to museums are ethics discussions about the myriad ways to handle collections—from their acquisition to their use to their occasional departure. For the most part, ethics involving what museums have in storage, on exhibition, traveling, or undergoing conservation are customary and acceptable. Questionable behaviors regarding collections can be subject to discussion inside the museum world and attract controversy outside it.

There are essentially three types of museums: art, science, and history. How they achieve their purposes are the same regardless of what they collect, own, and care for. Their content is proof for a subject the museum exists to study, preserve, and explain. Beneficiaries of that purpose can range from a small coterie of specialists to large and very general audiences. What sets museums in most nations apart from predecessor kindred undertakings is their civic nature. The vast majority exist for some shared contributory purpose beyond selfish individual pursuits. This idea evolved quickly when museums as we know them emerged. Art museum collections celebrate creative communications expressed visually. History museums hold the proof of people, places, events, etc. that happened years ago or yesterday. Science museums explore natural and scientific realms through objects relative to biology, chemistry, geology, physics, astronomy, the environment, and so on.

An organization's title need not include the word "museum" for it to be one. Thousands of operations are museums as commonly defined though they might be called a gallery, foundation, collection, society, or institute. Examples of these are the National Gallery of Art in Washington, DC; the Barnes Foundation in Philadelphia; the Frick Collection in New York City; the Maryland Historical Society in Baltimore, Maryland; and Historic Deerfield in Deerfield, Massachusetts.

Having established a generic functional definition of a museum, we recognize that individual museums always define their own persona in the form of a mission statement. These are short and general in nature. Some clearly explain the fundamental purpose of the museum in question. Others are more obscure and even grandiose. However they are written, ethics is usually not a word employed in a statement, though it might be implied. Museum mission statements can change over time as institutional priorities shift. This can have an impact on operational ethics, especially insofar as collections are concerned.

An ongoing debate that has been evolving for a few years involves El Museo del Barrio and its mission. Located on Fifth Avenue in Manhattan's old Spanish Harlem neighborhood, the museum was founded to promote the arts of Puerto Rico. At the time, the dominant population of Spanish Harlem was mostly from Puerto Rico. Over time, the museum has extended its scope to include contemporary Hispanic art from Central and South America. People bothered by this mission deviation are urging the museum to return to its roots. One of their demands for substantive change is "to expand the museum's collection of Puerto Rican art."[2] This debate illustrates how mission, ethics, and collections can intersect in problematic ways.

The mission debate hovering around El Museo del Barrio is not unusual when museums are accused of redefining a customary purpose. Such occasions happen rarely. Most museums in existence today do what they were originally established to do, but when they decide to radically, or even partially, change their missions, accusations of ethical violations are made by opponents. The ICOM call for museum definitions, noted in the opening quote of this chapter, received nearly three hundred responses from around the world. Some were quite specific in character while others were general. Consequently, no matter how similar museums might be, each is unique. Overarching ethical concerns for collections will reflect an operational singularity.

In Summary

Museum mission clarity is essential if the altruistic service aspect of these institutions is to be understood by supporters, not to mention the general public. Museums that are uncertain about what they are and why, inevitably suffer identity crises that lead to operational confusion and reputational disaster. Fortunately, most museums avoid this predicament. Ultimately, mission definition, adherence, and implementation rests with good governance. In the United States this is handled by volunteers usually known as a board of trustees. These are the people entrusted to assure the fiscal health and operating reliance of nonprofit entities. They select themselves. There are advantages and disadvantages to this system of charity governance. Chapter 2 explains and discusses the subject in the context of museums and their collections.

ETHICS IN ACTION

1. A museum was founded to preserve the heritage of a white immigrant group that once populated the neighborhood the museum is in. Since its creation, members of that demographic have gradually moved away. Today none remain in the area. The neighborhood is now populated by another immigrant group. It is not white. The board of trustees of the museum has decided it faces a mission dilemma since the "original constituency" of the museum no longer occupies the area. The new population has shown little interest in the museum. Most of its original supporters have died and few descendants identifying with the subject of the museum are involved with it. As it contemplates its future, what ethical considerations, if any, does it face as it evaluates its future?

2. A museum devoted to a subject learns it is the beneficiary of an important collection and substantial funding from a recently-deceased wealthy collector. She was from the area but had moved away years ago and never expressed any interest in the museum or the community since her departure. The collection is unrelated to the museum's mission. Many other museums would love to have it, and naturally, the ample funding that will accompany it. What should the museum do? How would ethics be involved in its response?

3. Who decides a museum's mission and how do ethics play a role in the decision?

Notes

1. International Council of Museums, "Creating a New Museum Definition—the Backbone of ICOM," December 19, 2019, http;//icom.museum/en/activities/standards-guidelines/museum-definition/.

2 Seph Rodney, "Has El Museo del Barrio Betrayed Its Mission?" Hyperallergic, May 21, 2019, https://hyperallergic.com/500266/el-museo-mission/?utm_medium=email&utm_campaign=Daily%20052219%20-%20Has%20El&utm_content=Daily%20052219%20-%20Has%20El+CID_52005ab2f65c25527611413a4fe59823&utm_source=HyperallergicNewsletter.

MUSEUM GOVERNANCE

The trustee's duty is to have the museum run, not to run it.[1]

he customary ownership authority for a private museum is usually referred to as a board of trustees. These individuals comprise the governance body and hold fiduciary responsibilities for the institution. They are self-appointed and must be held in the highest regard. Ethically they should avoid personal self-interest entanglements, especially where collections are concerned. To these ends, museums have founding documents that include articles of incorporation, bylaws, a mission statement, and recognition by the Internal Revenue Service for tax-exempt purposes. This chapter examines how museum trustees must behave in their civic capacity.

Museum Ethics Guides

To meet generally accepted ethical practices, museums have a variety of policies outlining staff and board expectations and requirements. These include a personnel manual, job descriptions, employment documents, and a code of ethics that will, or should, touch on collections in some manner. All must be formally and officially approved and updated when necessary by the board of trustees. The absence of written governing and operational directives signals a grievous ethical shortfall by a museum's board of trustees.

Exceptions to the stand-alone independent legal status for museums in particular would be those owned by governments, companies, or larger entities such as universities. These operations may have boards that serve in an advisory or fundraising capacity, but they rarely have any legal authority. Nevertheless, the ethical standards these museums aspire to usually mirror those of the mainstream museum sector rather than the larger entity of which they are a part. Unfortunately, unless these codes are officially accepted by the owning body and documented, in application they have superficial effect.

Trustee Ethics: Assumptions and Enforcement

Trustees are to support the best interests of the organization they govern rather than take personal advantage of their connection. Individual ethics profiles need to be unblemished in two personal arenas: their personal reputations in the world at large and their reputation within whatever charity they have volunteered to serve. The former reality is usually known by those who recommend an individual to be a trustee. The latter will be apparent after a person becomes a trustee.

The most immediate concern regarding trustee ethics requires avoiding obvious conflicts of interest. These can be defined in many ways. The easiest ones to note address financial arrangements that profit a trustee. This would be the case if a trustee is a lawyer who does paid work for the organization. The ethical behavior of trustees extends to their influence over collections. This is one reason most museums avoid having art and antiques dealers as trustees.

It is difficult to quantify how much has been written about the ethics charity organization board members must abide by. The books about ethics listed in the bibliography only partially touch on museum trustee behavior. This is particularly the case when it comes to collections. Examples of conflicts of interest are provided but overarching lengthy discussions of how trustees should act in their societal role is scant. Other options may prove more revealing. Presumably any study of nonprofit governance should reveal helpful definitions to be followed by boards of trustees for all sorts of charities, be they museums or not.

With the growth and refinement of the museum profession has come an increased understanding of the value and role ethics plays to assure esteemed institutional reputation qualities and daily operations. Those ethics are specific to the nature and needs of museums. Today many, if not most, independent American museums have reference codes of ethics. These are largely directed at employee behaviors. Collection duties are mentioned where and when relevant. How these codes apply to trustees differs from place to place. Some museums have trustee "job descriptions" that touch on ethics. Most do not. In fact, too often the good ethical behavior expected of board members is assumed rather than stated or required in any official way.

One common mechanism for reminding trustees of their need to be an ethically appropriate representative of a museum takes place annually when trustees are asked to submit conflict-of-interest disclosure forms, which have questions relating to possible or actual things a trustee may have done that could be misunderstood or that violates their implied duty to the organization on whose board they serve. When it comes to museum collections, trustee conflicts of interest might exist if a board member collects the same sort of items the museum collects, or if the trustee is a commercial dealer in those items, or if the board member is an artist whose work is in the museum on whose board he or she serves.

While exemplary ethical behavior is expected of museum employees, strict adherence to whatever norms an organization codifies may be less rigorously imposed on trustees. It is hard to give examples of violations that resulted in a person stepping down from a board. I directed two museums that had their endowments managed by trustee firms. No one complained about what, to me, was an obvious ethical breach. Only the eventual departure of the individual trustees resulted in changes of investment managers. In both cases, firms with no board connection were chosen.

Trustee service unfolds in social rather than corporate ways. Except as previously noted for government funders, no one is assigned by some authority to be a museum trustee. These individuals volunteer to be on a board and are elected to that service by that board. Presumably everyone knows what is expected of a candidate, including the candidate. These expectations can reflect various talents and abilities and also call for financial support.

When a trustee's contributions fall short, the person can be confidentially asked to leave a board. He or she may also voluntarily step down. However, it is not unusual for static trustees to remain on boards. This happens for several reasons, mostly social. These people usually know each other in a particular community and interact in ways unrelated to their museum context. They may have intertwining business associations, share places of worship, are congenial neighbors, or are relatives. It is highly unusual for trustees to leave boards for institutional ethics violations, or at least that is never a reason given publicly.

Trustee Ethics and Collections

When it comes to museum collections and trustees, the less these august personages are directly and intimately involved in how collections are acquired, cared for, studied, or used, the better. Rarely are trustees qualified to make substantive decisions about art, historic artifacts, or scientific specimens. This is not to say they are unintelligent or ill-educated. On the contrary; most museum board members are well educated and bright. Their volunteerism must leave collection judgments to directors, curators, collection managers, conservators, or knowledgeable consultants. The board's job is to assess that those employees implement the correct decisions and have the background to do so.

There are occasional examples of trustee transgressions insofar as museum collections are concerned. Recently in 2018, the board chair of a historic house museum bought a portfolio of prints by a living artist that show nothing related to the house, the site, or the mission of the organization. The suite of graphics is now in the collection. There was no acquisition involvement by staff, and no customary collecting review and approval process. The chair liked the artist. He bought the prints with his own money, which documents the value of the donation for his personal tax deductions.

Individual ethical deviations along the lines of the aforementioned take place with less frequency than in the past. It is the exceptional nature of this particular violation that makes it worth noting. Also, these irregularities may unfold mostly in small or new organizations that fail to understand or adhere to professional standards. Over time, collecting aberrations are an inevitable burden to museums. Bad acquisitions cost money to keep and maintain. They violate an organization's collecting purpose. Eventually they can be jettisoned, but that can have its own downside, such as time and money and can confuse public perceptions.

When museum trustees and collections intersect, the most prominent debates surround decisions to remove accessioned items. The practice of collection removal is almost as old as museums themselves, but in the 1970s it received alarming, if long overdue, public attention. The term "deaccessioning" was created to define this action and is discussed in chapter 11. Because trustees are the final decision-makers when it comes to subtracting collections, they must take responsibility for any ethical ramifications of the action.

Bad trustee behavior that occurs outside a nonprofit's circuit can be embarrassing or lead to the departure of the trustee. This happened twice at Seton Hall University in South Orange, New Jersey. In 2002, Robert E. Brennan's name was removed from a building when he was convicted of securities fraud. He was a major financial donor and had once headed the school's Board of Regents. A few years later, in 2005, Dennis Kozlowski requested that his name be removed from a building at the same university after pleading guilty to fraudulent financial dealings. While these examples are for a university, the same consequences can unfold at museums.

Over the years, the Museum of the City of New York has lost at least two "named" galleries. We can be sure that if anyone asked current trustees or staff, a quizzical look would be the response. Once upon a time there was the Arnold Galleries, named in honor of a lender of a large and important collection of pictures of New York City. When he died and it was discovered that he bequeathed the collection to the Metropolitan Museum of Art, the galleries mysteriously lost their identity. A few decades later, the Lucille Lortel Gallery was dedicated by herself in recognition of her influence in the New York City theater world. Today, there is no such gallery. Its name was lost during a construction project and never returned.

Trustee and Staff Collecting Ethics

Another area of concern involving museum collections and trustees unfolds with board or staff members who personally own or collect the same pieces collected by the museums they govern or work for. In the past, this was a less problematic conflation. Indeed, it was often considered a positive alignment of interests. Alfred Barr, the founding director of the Museum of Modern Art, had no difficulty advising trustees about new art to collect as he hoped it would someday end up in the museum's collections. On occasion this happened and on occasion it did not.[2]

Whether or not it is ethical for a trustee to collect the same sorts of items collected by the museum on whose board he or she serves is subject to debate. An argument in favor of the practice suggests such an individual is ideally suited to helping govern the museum in question because of their shared interests. Arguments against the idea rest on the conflicts that exist when two different collectors compete for the same things.

Concerns about museum trustee collecting conflicts extend to museum employees. Many museum personnel policies either forbid comparable collecting by employees or allow it if the museum gets right of first refusal on a possible private acquisition. This is an especially sensitive area for staff working with living artists exhibited by a museum or represented in its collection. Any private ownership of such an artist's work can be misconstrued. It suggests the artist enjoys a privileged relationship with the museum because of the gifting or discount sale of art to an employee with influence.

In 1967, an aspiring curator at a large urban art museum purchased an old painting that was first offered to the museum. The museum declined to take it. In his fledgling curatorial capacity, he saw the painting and met with the prospective donors. Once the institution passed on the acquisition, unbeknownst to it, he bought the item personally with the idea of selling it for a profit afterward. This was quickly revealed to the museum. Astonished at what it saw as a gross violation of professional conduct, the errant curator was allowed to step down. He then went on to be a very successful dealer in American art and antiques. Clearly his interests and talents were more suitable to this line of work. This sort of transgression was not referenced in any personnel policies or manuals as there were none at the time. It was simply understood to be "bad form." The initial secretive nature of the private sale suggested the curator knew this.

Today, acceptable and unacceptable job behavior is increasingly spelled out in employment documents. These are approved by governing authorities. What might have been considered an informal, "gentlemanly," mannered approach to operating a museum is long gone. If it ever really existed is questionable, given the ineptitude and overt racial, gender, and social discrimination that was too common. The professionalism that now enfolds museums has and continues to address matters of ethics that previously went either unrecognized or ignored.

In 2011, a museum in New Jersey presented an exhibit of metal toy banks owned by the husband of the chairwoman of the board. No one at the institution mentioned the obvious conflict of interest this action presented. The banks were not being given to the museum. The owner's name was flagrantly associated with the exhibit on-site and in all publicity. To the author's knowledge, the banks are still privately owned but their market value is now higher as a result of the exhibit.

The kind of museum trustee conflict of interest illustrated by the toy bank exhibit has been frowned upon for years. When it happens, it might celebrate a positive development for the hosting institution. An excellent case in point would be the October 20, 2014, to February 16, 2015, exhibit of Cubist art owned by Leonard A. Lauder, which was shown at the Metropolitan Museum of Art. The collection is a promised gift to the museum. The exhibit was essentially an announcement of this intentional donation. The works will fill a collecting gap for the museum, which was weak in this genre.[3]

It would be interesting to know if the trustees involved with either the toy bank or cubist collection noted this on their annual board conflict-of-interest disclosure form, assuming the museums with which they are associated require such documents. Frankly, having directed museums that used these disclosure forms, they appear to have zero meaning. They are filled out and filed in a museum office. The document is essentially a confessional that allows continued sinning. These documents have little substantive application.

In thinking about trustees and collection ethics, should an individual trustee have the unilateral authority to:

- acquire an object for a museum's collection?
- deaccession a particular object from a museum's collection?
- designate a museum collection object for conservation work, deciding what that will be, who will do it, when and how, and make the museum pay for the work?
- decide how a museum's collections can be accessed for research purposes?
- lend a museum object?
- hire collection staff?
- decide what object(s) a museum will exhibit, when, where, and how?
- be allowed to use a collection object for his or her private use?
- direct the museum to cover the costs of these actions?

These questions may seem hypothetical, but they are not. To assure a museum's ethical and professional collection protection, for the most part the answer to all these questions is a resounding NO. But, in practice they can happen. The best way to address potential violations is by establishing museum policies forbidding independent trustee meddling with collections.

Governance Ethics and Oversight by Nonmuseum Boards of Trustees

The ethical behavior of governing bodies responsible for museums should extend to boards of larger institutions if a museum is a part thereof. These most notably include college and university museums. There are many. Though the individual museums may have what appear to be boards of trustees, these usually have no, or minimal, legal authority. They are largely advisory in nature. Given the number and quality of college and university museums, their governance structure is operationally benign, especially insofar as collections are concerned or the ethical handling thereof. However, on occasion, problems can erupt. Two examples of questionable behavior (at least to the outside world) by school boards regarding museums held within their purview include actions by the trustees of Brandeis University, in Waltham, Massachusetts, and La Salle University, in Philadelphia, Pennsylvania. Both actions were legal.

In 2009, the board of trustees of Brandeis University announced it had decided to close the school's Rose Art Museum. Income from the sale of the collection would be used to strengthen the university's finances. The backlash from museum supporters, alumni, and other interested parties was strong enough to force a change in plans. The museum was retained, and no collections were disbursed.[4]

When the board of trustees of La Salle University announced plans to sell nearly fifty works of art from its museum in 2017, there was vociferous opposition (including a letter to the editor I wrote that appeared in the *Philadelphia Inquirer*). Opponent complaints fell on deaf ears and the sale proceeded as planned, at auction. The proceeds were used for the college's general fund.[5]

Governance Collection Ethics Accountability

I have neither witnessed nor heard of unethical trustee activities being publicly admitted to or resolved by museum boards. I have witnessed deceptive operating practices regarding endowment management, property expenses, collection acquisition and removal, and personnel favoritism. In these cases of obvious questionable behavior, no one was chastised or ushered off the board. The offending individual(s) might resign. Stated reasons for this action are always unrelated to an ethical transgression.

Deaccessioning is one action trustees might individually be publicly criticized for these days. The practice is a generally accepted museum collection management option, but on occasion, it can be quite controversial (examples are cited in chapter 11). Because voluntarily removing museum collections is ultimately a trustee decision, members of boards might be directly attacked by people who disagree with the idea. In these cases, boards understandably close ranks and leave media communications to museum directors or designated spokespersons. Still, given the community nature of museums, trustees cannot always avoid confrontations.

For the most part, at least in larger institutions, museum trustees take a hands-off approach to meddling in collection affairs. This is why the lion's share of museum collections have not been removed or mishandled. It is clear when announcements are made regarding new acquisitions, and the reasons are based on scholarship as promoted by staff. And, we see little trustee interference with exhibition creation and scheduling other than requiring adherence to set annual budgets or successful fundraising initiatives.

Ethics in the governance of museums must be clear, transparent, and agreed upon by all members of a board of trustees. This is especially important when it comes to the museum collections. A positive development in the past decade has been the development of opportunities for trustees to learn about their duties. There are now publications, workshops, retreats, panel discussions, etc. online and in person, about how to work together in a collaborative, productive, hands-off manner to the best advantage of a museum. The best way to learn about these is through the Museum Trustee Association at https://www.museumtrustee.org/.

In Summary

Summarizing the definition and overview of museum governance is necessary to assure both legal and ethical leadership. The public is the ultimate beneficiary of what a museum does. Some museums have a singular public while others have a plural public. Regardless, why and how a museum sets and meets its mission is obviously of immense importance. Because collections are the intellectual and practical center of these unique institutions, they are held in trust for past, present, and we hope, future generations. Trustees must understand and agree to this idea and ideal.

ETHICS IN ACTION

1. You attend an auction to bid on an object your museum wants to acquire. This has been preapproved by the collection committee of your institution and the full board. During the auction you see the husband of a board member bidding for the same object. What do you do?

2. You are the curator of a small historic house museum. The chairman of the board of trustees purchases an item to give to the museum. It is totally irrelevant to the mission of the institution. He tells the director to accept the gift, which the director does. The purchase and donation are a unilateral decision. It was never presented to any employee or trustee for consideration or official preapproval. What do you do?

3. A new director of a museum dislikes her predecessor who retired in good repute. After several years on the job, she decides to remove a small plaque honoring that director. It has been on public view without any dispute. Staff is perplexed at this development. What, if anything, should or could be done?

4. You are the director of a medium-sized museum. Unbeknownst to you, the board decides to create the position of chief operating officer. It does this without discussing the idea with you in advance. The discussion takes place at a special meeting of the board called specifically for this purpose. Though you have not been told to be absent, you are neither invited to, nor informed of, the meeting. It takes place at the museum while you are working. The candidate is your subordinate and is an unqualified employee who has been currying favor for at least a year with the most powerful trustee. What should you do?

Notes

1. Laurence Vail Coleman, *The Museum in America: A Critical Study*, Volume 2 (Washington, DC: The American Association of Museums, 1939), 390.

2. The practice is discussed at length in Alice Goldfarb Marquis, *Alfred H. Barr Jr.: Missionary for the Modern* (New York: Contemporary Books, 1989).

3. "Metropolitan Museum Announces Gift of Major Cubist Collection Comprising 78 Works by Picasso, Braque, Gris, and Léger from Leonard A. Lauder and Creation of New Research Center for Modern Art," press release, April 9, 2013, https://www.metmuseum.org/press/news/2013/lauder-announcement.

4. Randy Kennedy and Carol Vogel, "Outcry Over a Plan to Sell Museum's Holdings," *New York Times*, January 27, 2009, https://www.nytimes.com/2009/01/28/arts/design/28rose.html.

5. Eileen Kinsalla, "Outrage as La Salle University Forges Ahead with Plan to Sell Works from Museum's Collection, *artnetNews*, January 5, 2018, https://news.artnet.com/art-world/la-salle-university-decision-to-deaccession-artworks-sparks-outrage-1193042\.

ETHICS AND MUSEUMS

Museum ethics seeks to provide a purposeful, philosophical framework for all that the museum does.[1]

Today, ethics is a popular concern in the museum field. Once of peripheral interest, it is now a dominant topic embroiling what museums do and why. Ethics regarding race, gender, cultural identity, the environment, personal or group behaviors, morals, morale, and even legal issues, lurks in every aspect of museum work. Collections may or may not be a first focus of emerging deliberations, but inevitably they become central to conversations. This chapter suggests parameters that define museum ethics. It sets a baseline for the following chapters.

What Makes Museum Ethics Unique

Are museum ethics a unique concern, separate from ethics for other pursuits? Probably not. The sorts of ethical matters museums deal with are encountered by other human endeavors. Indeed, educational institutions, religious organizations, governments, the military, as well as the commercial and business world, all set and grapple with ethics. The overlaps with museums are simple. Acceptable or unacceptable conduct covers human relations, crime, questionable job incidents, and unbecoming employee behavior.

What segregates museums in the broad mix of workplaces is the role objects play in these endeavors; the tangible sets a defining framework for museums. Acquiring, owning, and caring for objects makes museums unique. This self-generated charge has caused the development of instructions, codes, procedures, policies, and directives tailored to specific museum ethics considerations.

An easy way to introduce museum collection ethics as a single subject is to walk through a customary acquisition process. Subsequent chapters dwell on this in more detail, but the following summary outlines institutional thinking and touches on the many questions that must be asked and answered for ethical as well as other reasons.

Museum Collection Ethics Process

Museum collecting typically unfolds in the following order:

- Acquisition discussions
- Acquisition approval
- Acquisition documentation
- Acquisition care
- Acquisition use

Acquisition Discussions

Before a museum begins acquiring for its collections, discussions must occur regarding the intellectual and practical nature of the purchase or gift or combination thereof. Questions have to be asked about the relevance of something to a museum's mission—is it ideal or ancillary to the work of an institution, are there entanglements that will or might encumber an acquisition, can the museum properly care for and use the object, does the potential acquisition present a conflict of interest, and does the institution have the resources to provide the sort of stewardship expected of a museum? Any failure to answer these and related questions positively presents an obvious ethical breech. Acquiring things in spite of negative responses to commonsense inquiries will burden the institution in the short and the long run.

Acquisition Approval

Ethically, the approval of a museum acquisition should be agreed upon by qualified staff and the board of trustees. Unilateral collecting by individuals is wrong in spite of any positive outcome relevance. Museums are not one-man bands. They are group undertakings. This is especially true when accepting collections. It is ethically questionable for either a trustee or employee to independently decide on what to acquire. An acquisition approval process must be documented in governance materials. These can be declared in meeting minutes as well as official collection management paperwork. Failure to meet this requirement is a governance ethical breech.

Acquisition Documentation

In addition to governance documents recording an acquisition, a museum must have in place a system for cataloguing what it holds for public benefit. This is usually the duty of a collection's manager or registrar, though in some cases curators, and even directors, might be involved. It is during this process that an object receives its accession number, an item's inventory identity that is unique to it. It is unethical to acquire collections and not catalogue them in accord with generally accepted museum practices. These may be different for archaeology materials, natural history specimens, art, or historic houses, but there are commonly agreed-upon systems for what might be considered disparate collections. Though duplicative, both hard copy and computer cataloging must be in place to assure ease of access and avoid information loss. The systems and locations must be secure.

Acquisition Care

When accepting a new acquisition, a museum is committed to providing safe and adequate physical care, usually for a prolonged time. "In perpetuity" is a popular phrase. It is a desirable concept rather than a reality. The idea supports a philosophical desire established by museums to acquire and hold collections forever. In practice, it is impossible to confirm the wish. Yet while some things museums own are removed on purpose or by forces over which they have no control, much of what museums have acquired over the years remains within them. How long this will last is anyone's guess. It is unethical to promise eternal care. It is equally unethical to suggest a cavalier ownership attitude to donors, employees, scholars, funders, or the general public.

In attempting to sustain the "in perpetuity" charge, museums work hard to protect collections. Considerable resources are devoted to proper storage, handling, and conservation, not to mention having employees trained and capable of attending to these duties. To collect and ignore such fundamental responsibilities is highly unethical.

Acquisition Use

Museums should collect with an intellectual purpose. To simply accept things haphazardly and let them occupy valuable space in storage, galleries, or other facilities is irresponsible. When obtained logically and for obvious reasons, collections will fulfill a number of uses. Their acquisition will be ethically sound as they are made available for research, exhibitions, image or physical reproduction, and other internal and external museum applications. For purely practical reasons, most museum collections are physically dormant whether on long-term exhibit or in long-term storage. This does not mean they are inaccessible or irrelevant. The digital age makes it readily convenient for scholars, artists, collectors, filmmakers, the general public, etc. to access museum collections for myriad uses. Such access depends on how well a museum has prepared collections to be seen online or in person. Often preapproval by the owning institution must be agreed to. Nevertheless, acquisition use is far easier in these applications than was ever the case. The ethics of how, for whom, when, and where use is provided must be decided upon by museum officials, but the ease with which it can be done is a quantum leap from previous challenges.

Museum Ethics Front and Center

For generations, Americans tended to see art museums as alternatives to crass everyday life. Like libraries, they were for learning; like churches, for reflection. You went to them for a hit of Beauty and a lesson in "eternal values," embodied in relics of the past donated by civic-minded angels.[2]

Whether about art, history, or science, if museums once enjoyed a certain innocence far removed from the hurly-burly of real life, that is no longer the case. Thoughts of the museum as an exclusive ivory tower were shattered during the social revolutions of the 1960s. (The notion was naive and debatable to begin with, but it certainly infiltrated common assumptions.) These august and intellectually removed temples of precious, curious, and odd things were suddenly called upon to shed their shyness. Museums had to be meaningful for all. This meant embracing demographic diversity however it was being defined. Museums were accused of gross ethical failures. They were called upon to redress past and present cultural, political, economic, and social ills, as well as various academic affronts. And, they had to maintain their function as places of celebration, memory, meaning, knowledge, and truth. (More about truth later.) It should have come as no surprise that the diverse personalities museums were forced to embrace, examine, and extol caused no little ethical consternation on the job.

To meet an astonishing list of new cultural assignments, museums began to embrace activities usually associated with nonmuseum entities and undertakings. Never before were museums so overtly expected to foster real estate development, become popular tourist attractions, act as economic catalysts, engage in a vigorous retail trade, or confer and promote social status. "To what extent museums should be places of entertainment has been a subject of heated debate for decades."[3] While these ancillary activities have not subsumed or replaced the core raison d'être of museums, which is explaining and proving subjects with original relevant objects, they have caused a far broader attention to be paid to museums than was once customary. The expanded expectations also resulted in operating revenues being shifted from collections to other pursuits. Some question the ethical validity of what they see as unrelated activities. They fight a losing battle. The museum as community center is now an accepted mission component.

When the new facts of museum life were unfolding, the people customarily responsible for museums were initially ill-prepared and even disinclined to admit change was necessary. They were unaccustomed to having assignments forced upon them from outsiders—especially if the outsiders were deemed ignorant about museums. Some museum leaders quietly engaged in rear-guard actions to deflect the inevitable. Over time, however, a new museology unfolded (appendix II).

Today, museums have to regularly justify their existence. In so doing, they must accept the fact that there can be perplexing reasons for public inquiry, criticism, and direction. That inquiry is often framed in ethics arguments. Is it ethical for a museum to do such-and-such and unethical if it does not? The nature of the such-and-such in question is almost immaterial. Collections have not escaped analysis. They must prove their worth in possibly ill-considered ways. They can be seen as a burden rather than a boon.

Since the 1970s, the resulting issues museums grapple with have had a positive effect on the ethics of institutional transparency, inclusiveness, and cultural sensitivity. Continued expectations or demands emanating from both inside and outside museums will result in continued change. Museums are far more accustomed to being quizzed, challenged, and investigated about all manner of actions. They are adept at offering inventive responses. When museums moved to what I call the center ring of the cultural circus, their public profiles became much more obvious.

Because collections are the DNA that defines museums physically and intellectually, accountability now focuses more sharply on them. Consequently, when museums are subject to controversy, it is no surprise that collections are a debate target. Institutional size, age, reputation, and geography make no difference when it comes to collection controversy. Small or large, rural or urban, old or new, famous or not-so-famous, every museum can be drawn into the maelstrom of collection ethics issues.

Museum Collection Codes of Ethics

Over the years, directives surrounding collections have caused museums to promulgate strictures about what they acquire and how those things are cared for and used. Self-generated guidelines are now spelled out in collection codes of ethics. Generally, these directives emerged from the field's professional membership organizations such as the American Alliance of Museums (AAM), the American Association for State and Local History, and the International Council of Museums (ICOM). Smaller and more discipline-specific museum-related organizations similarly evolved codes of behaviors. These now exist for registrars, fundraisers, conservators, and curators. We have seen individual museums galore write or subscribe to useful codes of ethics. One driving force in this regard has certainly been the AAM's accreditation program. Part of the process of becoming accredited involves having, or adhering to, an accepted professional museum code of ethics.

As with any documents created by diverse albeit related interests, there can be differences in content and consequences. Museum codes of ethics, especially insofar as collections are concerned, are no exception. Fortunately, there is enough unanimity in spirit to bind organizations into acceptable general agreements. We see this play out when collections are deaccessioned. Though the results of this subtractive action may not always reflect the spirit of most codes, the fact that the subject is even addressed is a remarkable positive step. Too often past actions by both museum trustees and staff saw collections as expendable. The idea that a museum had a preservation imperative when it came to the proper (however that might be defined at the time) care and use of these items was a foreign concept. Today, collection duties are understood, accepted, and even lauded. Codes of ethics are indicators of remarkable progress.

> Codes of ethics are intended to guide behavior and set standards of ethical practice. They are not laws, and, in fact generally call for standards of conduct higher than those set by laws. Professional codes of ethics are considered living documents because they continue to evolve in response to changing values, situations and social movements. For instance, both the ICOM and AAM codes have been revised several times. In this respect, we can see how ethical codes are relative to particular historical, social, national, and cultural contexts, just like ethical principles in general.[4]

Occasionally, museum staff ethics transgressions take place. Depending on the nature or frequency of a violation, the culprit is ushered out of the museum and usually leaves the profession. (This was certainly the case with two curatorial aspirants removed from a museum I directed years ago.) When a museum employee's ethical violation is also illegal, fines and/or imprisonment invariably happen. Fortunately, examples of this are few.

"When it comes to ethics in museums there are four core questions: What are they? Who has to abide by them? How can they be enforced? And, who must be held accountable?"[5] The issues regarding collections cover a great variety of concerns. While most seem to have to do with ownership, they also involve the care and use of collections. I suggest that as museums increasingly scrutinize how they get, keep, work with, and sometimes dispose of collections, conversations along the way need to focus on several potential or actual points of sensitivity. As discussed in subsequent chapters, I would include: acquisition, nondirect collection care, direct conservation, anticipated and daily use, exhibition application, interpretation/explanation, editorial/commercial use, collection access, deaccessioning, theft, and general standards.

An important note should be inserted here. In the late 1980s and early 1990s, when AAM was trying to update its previous code of ethics, there was a vociferous hue and cry from the field when the wording of a new draft was so strident and threatening that it appeared to suggest all museums were sinners until proven otherwise. Dire consequences would befall museums that failed to toe AAM's line. The result of the differences between the AAM draft and the museum profession at large resulted in the adoption of a fairly benign AAM code of ethics.

Given the sometimes ambivalent and personally opinionated nature of ethics, it is interesting to observe that few museums have been briefly or consistently seen as unethical operations. Regardless of bad or questionable practices, financial distress, and occasional staff dismissals, museums seem to continue to enjoy high levels of respect and veracity. There is a small but growing shelf of books about museum ethics (see bibliography). In the field, workshops, panel discussions, and lectures are starting to be presented on an array of ethics ruminations. Hard copy and online articles appear in both the museum trade press and related forums. These comments and declarations are positive. They certainly reflect the idea that museums (at least in democracies) ultimately answer to the general public, be they private or government operations. Some of this intercourse discusses collections but usually in a broader context separate from the full range of in-practice concerns. That needs to change.

In Summary

Museums have responded to the new attention on ethics with bureaucratic diligence. The subject is often referenced in museum policies. It is a popular topic of museum profession membership organizations. Individual museum employees are encouraged, or at least allowed, to express opinions on the matter. The outcome of diligent ethics conversations has been a positive development for museums generally. Attention to museum collection ethics as currently defined and applied will grow.

Traditional concerns will be added to with unimagined topics. What has been reviewed in this chapter encompasses known issues, but new ones are unfolding. While the future is promising, museums need to be aware of changes and nimble in how they embrace or reject accusations of ethical and unethical practices insofar as collections are concerned.

ETHICS IN ACTION

1. The museum you work for does not have a code of ethics for the institution itself. What, if any action, might you take regarding this circumstance?
2. In writing a code of ethics for a museum:
   a. Who should create it?
   b. What process might be followed (and by whom) to write, review, and accept it?
   c. What subjects should be included?
      • Define each.
      • Explain them in the context of a museum.
   d. Who will be responsible for monitoring compliance?
   e. What enforcement mechanisms will be in place?
   f. What are the consequences of violations?
   g. How will the code be updated, by whom?
   h. How will code changes be suggested and/or made?
3. What aspects of a museum operation might or should have its own code of ethics? And, how would that reflect or intersect with other institutional codes of ethics?
4. Will all museum codes of ethics be alike, or will there be differences according to museum types or specific institutional characteristics? For example, how might codes for art, history, and science museums differ, if at all?
5. Can a museum owned by another entity have its own code of ethics? If so, what body will approve it? Will the code hold any independent authority?
6. The director of a historic house museum overlooking the lower Hudson River, not far north of New York City, comments on what he considers the commercial value of pieces in the house when he gives a public talk about it. He was an antiques dealer prior to being hired by the historic house board of trustees. Are there any ethics implications to his lecture practice?

Without question, the one aspect of museums rarely dragged in the mud of ethical complaints rests with their collections. For the most part what museums own is what they say it is. Certainly, on occasion, a problem of authenticity or ownership legality can arise, but given the astonishing number of things in museums and their equally astonishing variety, they are to be complimented on the remarkably untarnished record of collecting, study, retention, and use for what they have and continue to seek. An insistence on collection veracity is what has caused museums to be so trusted by people. The following chapter delves into the essential character of this fundamental museum purpose.

Notes

1. Tristram Besterman, "Museum Ethics," chapter 26 in *A Companion to Museum Studies*, ed. Sharon Macdonald (United Kingdom: Wiley-Blackwell, 2010), 431.

2. Holland Cotter, "When Art, Money and Ethics Collide," *New York Times*, May 12, 2019, Arts & Leisure, 17.

3. Andrew Russeth, "The Ringmaster: Is Charles Venable Democratizing a Great Art Museum in Indianapolis—or Destroying It?" *ARTNews*, Summer 2019, http://www.artnews.com/2019/07/09/charles-venable-newfields-indianapolis -museum/.

4. Janet Marstine, ed., *The Routledge Companion to Museum Ethics: Redefining Ethics in the Twenty-First-Century Museum* (New York: Routledge, 2011), 80.

5. Steven Miller, *The Anatomy of a Museum: An Insider's Text* (Hoboken, NJ: Wiley-Blackwell, 2017), 241.

COLLECTION AUTHORITY

Artifacts in a museum carry with them the power of authenticity. Recent surveys find that people trust museums more than any other source of information. In part, that's because museums have real things. They offer, many visitors believe, direct, unmediated access to truth.[1]

The object-centric nature of museums relies on two essential characteristics: individuals who are specialists about certain collections and the intrinsic value of collection objects. Both hold authoritarian qualities. Ethical considerations swirl around them equally. This chapter discusses the authority of museum collections and those responsible for them. It touches on the meaning of what they acquire, care for, study, and show on behalf of a specialist or general public.

Museum Collection Trust

By the nature of their work and purpose, museums exude a sense of imposing credibility. This is first obvious in their very architecture. Years ago, they inhabited grand stone edifices often sporting Greco-Roman columned entrances and associated traditional design elements. Old majestic architecture is now supplemented or supplanted by arresting contemporary architecture. The museum as status symbol is all the rage. These civic temples have replaced cathedrals, majestic government buildings, or large, extravagant transportation centers as evidence of a place's importance. Around the world, new museums are being designed by famous architects. Each building stands out. Regardless of age, museum architecture declares they hold things of value, and those who run them are to be venerated for their altruistic contributions to society.

Inside museums their celebratory physical advertising continues. The sense of importance is obvious in "blockbuster" exhibitions, extensive security measures, and the vast array of precious things on display. Whether old or new, large or small, wealthy or poor, private or public, be they about art, history, or science, museum functions are all based on collections.

It is essential to understand and accept the idea that when it comes to collection authority, three actions must be interchangeably present:

- connoisseurship
- collecting
- curating

These inextricably blended pursuits have ethical contexts. Connoisseurship requires time to develop as a person learns about both the visual manifestation and the intellectual content of a subject. Unethical outputs of connoisseurship are ruinous as they foster informational lies about and false assessments of objects. Good collecting happens as a consequence of good connoisseurship. Wise curating is the outcome of insightful connoisseurship resulting in splendid collecting.

Individuals with Collection Authority

Curators are the individuals we most often think of when it comes to collection knowledge. Most have some subject specialty that is based on whatever objects they are responsible for or have been involved with over the years. It takes a long time to become recognized as an authority in a particular area. Good curators are of immense value for a museum's reputation and its contents. Weak or bad curators have the opposite effect. Because curators interact both physically and intellectually with collections, they must recognize, agree with, and abide by strict ethical constraints both on and off the job. These are clearly listed in the American Alliance of Museums' (formerly American Association of Museums) Curators Committee, Code of Ethics for Curators (appendix III). The emphasis in the code is almost entirely collection relevant and related. For the purposes of this discussion, authority is considered synonymous with being an expert or specialist in a particular museum collection or collections.

Curators are usually full-time museum employees, but there is a growing coterie of freelance curators. Lately this has been especially so for specialists in contemporary art. With the advent of major art fairs, non-collection-based art centers, and modern art dealer–organized exhibitions around the globe, they comprise a transient international group. Depending on qualifications and contract arrangements, the competence and value of independent curators equals that of museum curators. The ethical questions raised by the difference in employment circumstance touch on suspicions that museums find it cheaper to hire independent curators for temporary assignments such as organizing exhibitions and catalogues or for special research projects. The cost of these people is less than might be the case for full-time personnel. Museums need to be watchful when freelance curators work with an institution's permanent collection. Regardless of qualifications, they should not have final unbridled authority regarding ownership, storage, access, or conservation decisions.

Occasionally, a museum director will also be a person who is an authority on some aspect of a collection. This is not as common as it used to be. The age of the director-curator is almost entirely a thing of the past, at least in the United States. Administrative duties now consume the lion's share of a director's schedule; he or she has little time for sustained scholarship, be it research, writing, organizing exhibitions, or the like. Many directors may have begun as a curator or subject specialist, but those interests are difficult to pursue once a person becomes a museum director. If a director is performing curatorial work, as sometimes happens, it is always at the expense of responsible museum management.

Regardless of which museum position holds authority over a collection or an aspect thereof, ethical concerns must be acknowledged. To begin with, is the individual actually the specialist he or she purports to be? Occasionally, someone claiming authority, or being given authority, is totally unqualified for the assignment. The author encountered such a curator at a museum he directed years ago. The person posed as knowledgeable but upon further investigation was not. The first indication was the discovery of his lying about having a bachelor's degree. Fortunately, this happens very rarely in the museum field. The vast majority of experts regarding collections are ethically forthright. And, they have the requisite academic and experiential credentials to prove it.

Collecting mistakes can prove especially pernicious when museum employees with no knowledge of a particular subject or objects make an obvious acquisition error. A former director of a New Jersey museum did this some years ago when she unilaterally accepted into the permanent collections three alleged Salvador Dali prints one December when the donor needed a last-minute tax deduction. Dali is one of the most counterfeited artists in the world. The donation offer should have raised an immediate red flag because the prints had been purchased on a cruise from a shipboard shop run by the Park West Gallery of Southfield, Michigan. Even a cursory investigation would have shown the gallery was embroiled in lawsuits for selling questionable Dali prints.[2]

The ethics of individual collection authorities infuses the realm of what they know and say about the objects for which they are responsible. This is essential for museums to continue to be places of truth. Collection veracity presumably is known at the time of acquisition when information causing the action is thought to be correct and current. Of course, mistakes will be made, but expertise is usually sound. When errors are discovered, museums need to make them known and let records reflect the new information.

Who decides who has collection authority? Are these experts self-anointed or is their standing independently corroborated? Most collection authorities gain their knowledge incrementally over time. It has to grow from constant and direct interaction with whatever things one knows well. It is a slow and deliberate process of reading, looking, thinking, exploring, and being creative seekers of information on many fronts as well as open to unanticipated discoveries.

How long can collection authority last? For some, it is a lifetime. For others it is temporary, as happened to me when I was senior curator at the Museum of the City of New York. In addition to management assignments, I was responsible for an extensive and fabulous collection of paintings, prints, and photographs. In that capacity, I took a special interest in the lithographs of N. Currier and Currier & Ives. These were produced in the mid-nineteenth century and the museum owned about three thousand of the firms' prints. When I changed jobs and moved on to other museums, my standing as an expert in this subject declined. Though for a while I continued to give slide lectures, the loss of direct and regular access to the collection ended the ongoing research I was once able to pursue. In retrospect, how ethical would it have been for me to claim to be an expert when I was so removed from the original art?

What ethical thoughts or actions need to be considered by collection authorities? Additional ethical concerns surrounding voices of authenticity are about words used to supply information. Language must be honest and clear. Verbal obfuscation and esoteric words only confuse and perplex. Art and antiques dealers seen on the popular television series *Antiques Roadshow* often mention patina when speaking about a piece of sculpture or furniture. Patina is the physical surface condition and appearance of an object. A rule of thumb in today's market is, if something of value has what is thought to be "the original patina," it is worth more than if the surface had been altered since the item was made. In most cases it is fairly apparent if a chair, cast bronze figure, or chest-on-chest has had its surface changed. So what? Do we really, actually, and without question know something is as it was when made two hundred years ago? Original patina can have many meanings.

In the art and antiques trade, ethics is a slippery slope. While the vast majority of dealers attempt to be honest in their business, museum involvement needs to be pursued with institutional eyes wide open. In addition to the silliness about "original patina" are concerns regarding provenance. Unless a dealer is selling an old painting, chair, carpet, lamp, etc. that has a verifiable specific ownership history, the source of an object is couched in generic terms: "It came from a private home in New England." "It was owned by a prominent collector." "We purchased it at auction some years ago."

Because museum collections provide evidence of a subject or some aspect thereof, provenance is a core acquisition consideration. Where an object came from, who made it, who used it and how, and has it changed since its making, are all critical pieces of information sought during a collecting process. This applies to some art, most historical artifacts, and various categories of scientific specimens. Commercial dealers can be quite secretive when it comes to divulging provenances as they want to keep their sources confidential. In the case of art, this may not matter (unless a piece has been stolen), but with artifacts and science items it may be an unfortunate lapse. Is it ethical for science or history museums to acquire objects with no verifiable scholarly provenance?

Can a collection authority be scuttled? Yes. Sadly, the worst examples of attacks come from within museums themselves as happens when someone in power decides an expert is dispensable. This can occur for several reasons, none of which are entirely ethical. I can offer two examples.

While writing this book, a regional art museum in Pennsylvania fired a superb curator because a couple of board members didn't like her. She opposed their curatorial interference when they insisted on purchasing a second-rate painting for the collection. They did not understand the value or importance of her scholarship, which was clearly apparent in her fine exhibits and research. This was a textbook example of trustees pretending to have curatorial expertise. Though there are exceptions, few trustees are even remotely qualified.

The Western Reserve Historical Society has a terrific costume collection. I was introduced to it when I was director of the museums there in the first half of the 1990s. The curator knew the collection extremely well. He was a stellar resource for explaining how the contents reflected the region's historical might, as seen through the industrial wealth that afforded the purchase of stylish couture, design, and fashion by wealthy Cleveland women. A few years after I left the society, a new CEO fired the curator for failing to get to work on time.

Instances of ethical wrongdoing by mismanagers disrupting quality museum operations are legion. The worst damage tends to play out on the governance and directorial levels. Eventually, the damage is recognized and corrected, but the adverse impacts upon individuals and the institution are long lasting. The ethical standing of the suffering museum is sadly diminished. Certainly, employees with minor administrative and management authority can cause damage. This was the case with a maintenance person I hired once. Retaining these employees is, ultimately, the fault of higher-ups—including me.

Though examples are rare, occasionally a collection specialist is found wanting for legitimate intellectual reasons. The loss of status is never publicly announced. The museum and scholarly world are quiet about peers and colleagues being denied a long-held rank. Faith in a person's knowledge essentially evaporates. A key accusation is that the individual acted in an unethical manner. We see this play out in the business world on a regular basis. The #MeToo movement has heightened awareness of ethical sexual misbehavior in the workplace.

Authority Collections

For whatever reason, certain things, works of art in particular, have long enjoyed a unique celebrity status. This has always been the case, even before museums existed. Their renown gives them an unparalleled intrinsic authority. That meaning varies according to viewer prejudices and what respected authorities say over time. Vacillating commentary aside, the respect and admiration star items receive places them on a special level of appreciation.

It is difficult to know why certain things are admired to the degree they are. Suffice it to say, this is a reality that museums must cope with when they are the keepers of an "authority object." Given the informational, emotional, and cultural value museums ascribe to their collections, these objects take on a certain authority when they assume a new role in life as a museum collection piece. For the most part, institutions gladly accept this duty. A few obvious examples of authority collection objects would include Leonardo da Vinci's painting *Mona Lisa,* the ancient Greek statue known as the *Venus de Milo*, the ancient Egyptian *Rosetta Stone*, and Van Gogh's 1889 painting *Starry Night* (figure 4.1).

While access to and conservation of museum collections is always an ethical duty, these two concerns are heightened with major authority objects. How can people see a famous work of art without discomfort to themselves or the object of their attention? Crowd control is necessary, and that is usually handled with security personnel on duty in the display area. Protections must be in place to guard against or reduce the impact of vibration that might occur because of earthquakes or outdoor nearby traffic and similar physical dangers. Assaults during war and civil unrest may be difficult to avoid, but protective plans need to be made nevertheless.

The conservation aspect of collection care addresses the environment in which objects are kept as well as direct actions taken to and on those objects. Because authority objects are so famous, they may tend to

Figure 4.1. Van Gogh's 1889 painting *Starry Night* on exhibit at the Museum of Modern Art, New York City. It is the most popular object in the museum's galleries. For security and viewing comfort a guard is on duty to keep people from crowding around the picture too closely. Photo by Steven Miller © 2018

receive more attention than other things a museum owns. Climate control for temperature, humidity, air quality, and light levels is always created to optimal effect and monitored. But other conservation measures include assuring the safety of how a piece is displayed whether on a wall, on a pedestal, hanging from a ceiling, or setting on a floor.

Is it ethical to devote more attention to authority objects than those less in public demand? That question can only be answered by the museum owner. Typically, it is a matter of public relations. The ethics of fame are fickle. God forbid *Starry Night* would inadvertently fall off the wall it hangs on, or suffer from attack by a crazed visitor, or be hit with too much damaging direct light. Unless there were oddball unanticipated reasons for such actions, the critics would have a field day and rightly so.

To be sure, large, famous museums with globally significant collections are not alone when it comes to owning authority objects. Smaller institutions can face the same circumstance. The Bennington Museum in Bennington, Vermont, has a quilt that is venerated by quilt lovers internationally. Known as the *Jane Stickle Quilt*, it was made during the American Civil War (1861–1865). This fact was noted on the quilt by its maker with the date 1863. Fabric can be extremely light-sensitive. The quilt is in good condition. To meet its preservation imperative and to support what it feels is an ethical obligation to make collections available to the public, the museum exhibits it briefly once a year.

Most museum collections hold content authority. As noted, however, the quality of that authority will vary. A pair of old shoes in a costume collection may be of negligible value if it was commonplace when worn, it is represented in many museum costume collections, and the owner is unknown. The importance of those shoes would change if they were rare survivors of a particular time period and the owner was famous. The nature and provenance of the shoes will have an impact on the magnitude of their authority. Yet that authority is entirely subjective. The ethics surrounding these considerations vacillate accordingly. Some might think it is unethical to devote the collection management resources required to keep ordinary shoes, while others will say their ordinariness is precisely what makes them important. Objects are given authority by authority figures.

In Summary

"The point of collections and museums, it is no exaggeration to say, revolves around the possession of 'real things' and . . . it is essentially this which gives museums their unique role."[3] As explained, deciding what "real thing" is of such intrinsic or associative value as to warrant being in a museum depends on judgments about an item's aesthetic, historic, or scientific information. Customarily, this subjective exercise is assigned to designated authorities. Museum staff positions given this job are usually curators, but they can also be scientists, historians, specialist consultants, or directors. Some objects are obviously important, as might be the case with a Rembrandt etching, while others gain importance, as has happened over the past few years with art created by African American painters. Given the attention museums assign collections, how they are treated in these institutions is of the upmost importance. The following chapter delves into this essential responsibility.

1. A small local historical society has for years exhibited a circa 1880 buffalo-skin coat worn by a resident of that community but long after he left the area permanently. Descendants of the former resident (who also live far away from the area) donated the coat fifty years ago. The original owner was a graduate of the United States Military Academy at West Point and was in the U.S. Cavalry during the so-called Indian Wars in the north central part of America. It was during that time that he acquired the coat. Exhibit label copy succinctly identifies the owner of the coat, its donors, and his military history. What ownership or exhibit ethics issues might there be for this authentic object?

2. The Bennington Museum owns a large American flag that is arguably the second most famous one in the nation. The first is obviously the one owned by the Smithsonian Institution that flew over Fort McHenry in Baltimore harbor and inspired Francis Scott Key to write the national anthem during the War of 1812. The Bennington flag is notable for the numeral 76 in the blue canton in its upper left corner. When the flag was acquired by the museum, the director at the time claimed it was flown at the Revolutionary War Battle of Bennington (which actually took place in nearby Hoosick, New York). Subsequent scholarship rejects this idea and suggests it dates from the time of the centennial of the United States in 1876. The condition of the flag is delicate as the colors have faded and the material is fragile. The museum has exhibited it in a large gallery with ample light for years. The museum feels an obligation to display the item. Twenty years ago a major textile conservation project was conducted to clean and secure it from further degradation. The work was done by a highly qualified textile conservation center. What ethics issues might involve this national icon?

3. You are the curator of art collections in a Jewish history museum. There is a watercolor image of an Austrian street scene painted by Adolph Hitler. Hitler aspired to be an artist but was rejected twice when he applied to art school in Vienna. Eventually he gave up the idea of an art career. The painting had been donated to the museum by a concentration camp survivor whose father ran an art gallery that purchased small paintings by Hitler. What ethics concerns would surround this work in the museum's collection?

4. You are the director of a regional history museum. A curator you have recently hired is doing an assessment of one of your most important collections. She has determined much of it is unrelated to the museum's mission. The region was known for making a distinctive sort of pottery in the mid-nineteenth century. That style of pottery was also made by other ceramic manufacturers well beyond your location. Over the years, the museum has been given several thousand pieces whether made locally or not. The curator has researched the difference extensively and now recommends the wholesale deaccession of the nonregional pieces. You agree and the board concurs. The deaccessioned pieces are sold through an auction house specializing in ceramics. The museum's name is associated with the sale and information on why is noted in a media release. An individual proclaiming expertise in the ceramics being sold takes issue with the museum's decision. He has no affiliation with the museum but makes his opinion prominently known in trade publications both online and in hard copy. What ethical concerns should the museum have, if any?

5. You are the new director of a regional history museum. Not long after starting your job you hear rumors that the museum's curator (the only one) might not have an undergraduate degree. He makes no claim to a graduate degree but says he attended a particular university, and this is listed on grant applications that require information on staff academic profiles. The curator claims no scholarly background and his work, while adequate, falls short on certain scholarly levels. He never talks about his schooling. In time, and after further suggestions that he does not have a college degree, you call the university he claims to have attended. In asking when he graduated, they say he has not and needs to complete about fourteen more hours to get his degree. You then call the previous director. She is aghast at the information you have uncovered. Apparently, when she hired the curator, another candidate was so incensed she complained to the director that the curator had no undergraduate degree. The then director asked the curator, and he said he only had to complete a few courses, such as gym. That summer he took two months off to do that. When he returned to the museum, he told the director all was well and his degree was on its way. She asked if she should check with the school, but he said that was unnecessary. Ethically, how should you, as the current director, handle this situation?

Notes

1. Steven Lubar, *Inside the Lost Museum: Curating, Past and Present* (Cambridge, MA: Harvard University Press, 2017), 164.

2. Vernon Silver, "Ever Bought Art on a Cruise? Prepare to Be Seasick," *Bloomberg Businessweek*, December 14, 2016, https://www.bloomberg.com/news/features/2016-12 14/ever-bought-artwork-on-a-cruise-prepare-to-be-seasick.

3. Susan M. Pearce, *Museums, Objects, and Collections: A Cultural Study* (Washington, DC: Smithsonian Institution Press, 1992), 24.

5

MUSEUM COLLECTING METHODS

The chase and the capture of a great work of art is one of the most exciting endeavors in life—as dramatic, emotional, and fulfilling as a love affair.[1]

Understanding museum collecting methods is essential when discussing museum collection ethics. This chapter explains several ways museums acquire what they own. It reviews desirable institutional and individual motivations, conduct, and practices to achieve untarnished behaviors by museums. Of equal importance, these need to be known by people outside institutions from or through whom collections are obtained.

The Three Museum Collecting Methods

What we see in museums is acquired in one of three ways: donations, purchases, or field collections. These arrangements and combinations thereof will continue to be the norm. From negligible to considerable, ethics considerations infuse all processes.

In the United States, the vast majority of what history and art museums hold was donated to them. Archaeology holdings mostly result from field excavations undertaken by the owning museum or deposited with it in some official capacity by an authorized entity unaffiliated with the museum. Natural history museum collections are also field collected, either by scientists working independently or for a museum.

Museum collection gifts are made by living donors or through bequests by the recently deceased. Companies, clubs, schools, and governments also give things to museums. Occasionally, something is placed in a museum for safekeeping by an outside authority such as a federal, state, or local agency, but these are exceptional circumstances and often temporary. They are loans.

Occasionally, objects become museum collections when they are in a place that later becomes a museum (as is often the case with historic houses). This collecting method would fall into the gift or purchase method of acquisition. The ethics of such a transition will vary according to the purposes of the action. For example, when the contents of a historic house shift from private to public ownership, they can be subject to the same sort of retention scrutiny all museum collections receive, either when being considered for acquisition or when being reviewed for retention. These deliberations must include ethics discussions. The original intent of the establishment of a historic house museum may or may not require holding everything contained in the new museum. If not, is it ethical to dispose of unwanted materials?

Collection purchases are made with money a museum has set aside for this purpose and/or with funds donated for a purchase. Many museums have acquisition budgets though they may be small. This is cash restricted exclusively for buying art, artifacts, or scientific specimens. Sometimes this money is designated for a specific object category. These could include prints, furniture, cars, fossils, photographs, costumes, or minerals, to name a few. A targeted collecting agenda indicates a museum or donor is focused on a specific area of object interest and is underwriting its commitment with money. To spend funds restricted to collection purchase for another use is unethical.

Museum Donor Motivations

People give things to museums for many reasons. The vast majority do so because of an interest in the mission of a particular museum. Thus, someone with an old car might be inclined to give it to a car museum. People owning antique clothing might give the material to a textile museum. Or, descendants of an important furniture maker might wish to give a chair by that maker to an appropriate museum. Collectors are logical donors to museums. But, much of what is acquired is a single object given by an individual. It is argued sometimes that people donate to museums simply to create personal tax deductions. Certainly, few donors decline to take advantage of this option, but it is hardly their first donation reason. The vast majority of collection donations raise no ethical concerns. However, conflicts can happen, and museums must be on guard regarding not just the nature of an object but why it is being given.

Whether donating an item or money to purchase it, whoever makes the contribution and what their motivations are can range from a dull to a fascinating subject. Sometimes it can be a suspicious arrangement. A donor might be taking advantage of an institution's charitable status to inflate his or her social standing, to get a beneficial tax deduction, or to foist off stuff they no longer want, which the museum may or may not want. Of course, if the museum wants the donated object, personal inclinations might be immaterial.

Customary Art and History Museum Collecting Concerns

Museums prefer object donations to be unencumbered by restrictions. However, there are several restrictions that people may require. Some will demand that an object be on constant exhibit and in a certain place. Though ethical to do so, this is extremely unwise for long-term operational as well as conservation reasons. Donors can insist on having a right of return if an item is deaccessioned in the future. This is to be avoided, and it is often impractical when generations change and designees die or are otherwise impossible to locate. Donors can request the occasional loan back of a piece for their private if temporary use. This is a totally unethical idea. Donors may want to attach restrictions on how research is conducted about an object, or what conservation measures may or may not be done. Occasionally, a museum donor may want to make his or her gift over time. In other words, an object will be donated incrementally on a prearranged schedule. Twenty percent might be donated per year for five years before the museum will own the object in its entirety. In addition to the practical and preservation concerns of such an arrangement, legal counsel will be necessary to opine on the wisdom of the idea, including where the object will reside during the process.

All too often museums have to justify how and why they collect and what can or cannot be done for donors. At the top of this list of protocols is the museum profession's practice to avoid giving monetary appraisals for donations. The Internal Revenue Service frowns on this. Museums can suggest appraisers for donors to contact and usually a list of at least three is suggested. The personal financial business of museum donors is none of a museum's business.

The media loves to feature stories about expensive collection purchases. Even if the acquiring museum has not divulged what was paid, in most cases it is easy to estimate a market value. For ethical reasons, museums avoid discussing monetary assessments for collections. Though some list their acquisitions as financial assets and capitalize holdings in annual reports, public numbers summarize a solo figure for entire collections. They are not exactly guesstimates but hardly correspond to precise current market values. For example, a museum holding Early American furniture would have to reassess values set twenty years ago for chairs, tables, sideboards, corner cupboards, beds, etc. because the market for these things has dramatically declined in the past two decades.

Museums have collection insurance, but the cap in no way reflects the total current retail replacement cost. It is for partial loss as museums almost never lose all their accessioned items at once. These are occasionally updated as museum collections grow and if highly valued items or whole new collections are acquired. It should be noted there is nothing unethical about either capitalizing collections or declining to do so. An institution's official methodology of collecting can embrace or reject this.

In addition to celebrating important collection purchases, the press will also herald major gifts. Announcements appear with some regularity in both the general news and a host of trade outlets both in hard copy and online. Exhibition object labels confirm the fact that outright donations are the most common form of museum collecting. The vast majority have a credit line for the item's donor. When organizing a collecting method, how that public acknowledgment is to be stated, if it is to be stated, must be noted.

Science Museum Collecting Methodologies

Science museums tend to fall into two institutional categories: natural history and archaeology museum. Collections are acquired by gift or purchase, but much is gathered by employees themselves. This unfolds when scientists and others bring in natural history flora and fauna specimens to study and retain for research purposes, as well as for public exhibition and information. Archaeology excavations conducted by staff amount to masses of materials including samples of the earth objects were found in. Museums can also be designated official repositories for findings from digs conducted by nonstaff. These sorts of acquisition activities might be categorized as a form of purchase if the museum itself is paying for the work. However, those costs rarely appear as acquisitions expenses in an annual financial report. They are not hidden, just listed elsewhere, usually as part of general operations. Ethics regarding the methods of getting, keeping, and using archaeologically excavated material are increasingly under scrutiny by special interest groups outside museums.

There are considerable ethics debates about the act of archaeology collecting. They start with who has the right to excavate where, when, and how. There has long been a divide between prehistoric archaeology and historic archaeology. This division is melding as Western definitions of peoples changes for various cultural reasons. Populations previously called illiterate, primitive, or backward are now accorded more respect and might be generically identified as indigenous, tribal, native, or accorded titles reflecting places of origin or excavation discovery. Except for Northern European groups, these ancient populations tended to be non-Caucasian racially.

Once, archaeologists (who were largely white and from Western countries) could pretty much dig where, when, and how they wished, sometimes getting (paying for) permission from local authorities and avoiding areas of conflict. They tended to keep what they found. The good stuff was removed to their home countries. These approaches to archaeology are fairly passé. Ethical questions galore emerged to alter past practices. From a collecting perspective, less is removed from countries where specimens are found. Sharing might be arranged. Archaeology teams increasingly include representatives of native citizens and academics. How discoveries are announced, saved, and made available to the general public is different than was the case fifty or a hundred years ago. These changes all result from adjusted thoughts in the ethics of archaeology.

Alterations in how archaeology is pursued today include what is sought for more modern eras. Sites of interest dating back a hundred or two hundred years ago may be treated in ways previously unheard of. This is especially the case with human remains. For example, American Indian or African American burial sites are now subject to changed approaches when it comes to digging. Permission from representatives of these groups, however identified, is sought before the first trowel of earth is overturned. Monitoring of a project can continue from beginning to end. And, how to deal with what is discovered is of immense ethical importance. Human remains are not shown as often in museums as was once the case.

Natural history collecting can be rife with ethics debates. On the surface, acquiring representative flora and fauna for museums might appear to be a benign pursuit. In practice, scores of problems can erupt such as legal entanglements in getting specimens that are rare, protected, or endangered. The debates can happen in the United States and globally. Various countries have different laws about what can or cannot be taken, how, by whom, when, and under what circumstances.

A paper published recently in the *Journal of the British Tarantula Society* about the discovery of a new species of spider "claimed that the researchers had received their specimens secondhand from private collectors in Poland and Britain, who had poached them in Malaysia."[2] The researchers claimed they had the correct local permits to have their specimens. The journal declined to retract the article. However, "the incident has reignited a decades-old debate about research ethics, specimen collection and 'biopiracy'—the use of natural resources without obtaining permission from local communities or sharing any benefits with them."[3] "No one knows how prevalent illegal collecting and use of poached specimens is among scientists, not only because of the covert nature of this trade, but also because it can be hard to define who counts as a scientist and what counts as breaking the law." "The ethics surrounding scientific acquisitions can be hazy."[4]

Museum People Responsible for Collecting Methods

As previously explained, only a few designated museum positions are involved in collecting. For art and history museums, they are largely directors and curators. Science museum collecting is established by scientists on staff and sometimes in the field. These posts may or may not hold the title of curator. A few may not even be academically trained or recognized professionals.

A museum will often have a collection committee made up of trustees, staff, and possibly outside experts. Their work is to review, approve, or deny acquisitions. The final role of trustees is to confirm for the official record decisions made by a collection committee or staff. Most boards are unqualified to initiate acquisition proposals. Trustees generally have neither the knowledge nor the requisite expertise regarding museum collecting as previous lax and faulty practices in this regard document.

Great curators are avaricious when it comes to collecting. They nurture, solicit, cultivate, finagle, lure, and otherwise do their best to bring in whatever they believe is and will continue to be important evidence of their subject specialties. When judiciously and carefully pursued, curatorial acquisition refinement results in treasure troves of valued holdings. Billions of things are owned by tens of thousands of museums, ultimately for public benefit. This will continue. "When collections cease to grow they begin to decay. A finished museum is a dead museum, and a dead museum is a useless museum."[5]

Given the number of things still in museum collections that arrived in years past, the acquisition track record of curators is pretty good. Naturally, they sometimes falter. For long-standing museums, especially history museums, most irrelevant items arrived when collecting was less disciplined and focused. Ethics concerns regarding museum acquisitions can range from severe to none. Some objects will predictably elicit highly incendiary feelings while others cause no adverse reactions. Museums are usually aware of any positive or negative sentiments that might accompany an acquisition. Sometimes disgruntled responses are unpredicted. Museums love to extol exciting collecting news, and media information is disseminated in a timely and extensive manner. Unexpected adversity will require a fast and honest reply.

In practice, the usual procedure for collecting at a museum follows one of two courses: A museum person in authority, such as a curator or other specialist, expresses a desire to acquire an object for a museum; or someone outside a museum offers an object of interest. In either case, a collecting proposal should be made and reviewed by appointed staff and possibly qualified volunteers. It is increasingly common for museums to have collection committees to review all manner of acquisitions. These committees can be made up of staff only, volunteers only (including trustees), or a combination thereof.

Typically, the board of trustees will approve the final acquisition decision. It can do this in a pro forma manner by simply accepting staff and/or committee recommendations, or by having an informed presentation and discussion. Once an acquisition decision is made, the donor or seller is notified and the proper paperwork is completed for the gift or sale. The actual transfer of the object could already have occurred (with loan documentation) or it will happen when the acquisition process is formally and officially concluded. The physical transfer is part of that process. These steps comprise the common and appropriate collecting methods of most responsible professional museums today.

It is important to note that the collecting methods outlined here may or may not pertain at museums operated by universities, individuals, or companies. These organizations can have different approaches to collecting. For instance, a museum owned by an individual(s) but open to the public may acquire only what the individual wants. He, she, or they will make any and all decisions. Collecting is therefore a private and unilateral endeavor. In the case of colleges and universities, there may be ancillary offices or appointees involved with a decision-making acquisition process. These individuals or groups will be appointed by school authorities.

Acquisition Documentation Methods

In discussing collecting ethics, the requirement to have proper gift or purchase documentation is of the utmost importance. It is essential to explain and understand for any collecting method to be valid. Extensive and helpful museum procedures are in place and are explained in detail in pertinent collection management publications. Foremost among these is *Museum Registration Methods,* 5th edition, edited by Rebecca A. Buck and Jean Allman Gilmore.[6] To briefly extrapolate, documentation should include a written and photographed description of an object, signed and even notarized ownership transfer authority, and copies of ancillary documentation.

In Summary

Museum collecting methods pose a wide range of ethics concerns. Institutions need to exercise care regarding ownership legalities, provenance, relevance, storage, conflicts of interest, conservation requirements, and use capabilities, to name the most pressing subjects. Thousands of things are acquired every year by museums. For the most part, this activity causes no ethical conundrums. In fact, it fulfills an essential museum commandment. Virtually every definition of these institutions includes their self-mandated charge to collect. The preservation imperatives

1. The children of a recently deceased amateur "pot-hunter" who dug up American Indian ceramics in New Mexico wants to donate them in his memory to the local historical society in the area where the man did his digging. The children want to make their donation over a period of ten years. As the curator of the historical society, what ethical concerns would you have regarding this offer?

2. A member of the board of trustees of the museum you direct wants to donate money for the purchase of a work of art for the museum that is of no interest to the museum. There are no known conflicts of interest regarding the trustee's interest in or association with the art, its market, or collectors of this sort of work. The trustee is wealthy. She has served on the board for years and is admired by other board members and the community generally. What ethics circumstances surround this proposal?

3. The museum that you direct has been approached by the local police department, which offers to donate the AR15 assault rifle used in a massacre that killed eighteen students at a local high school. The gunman was killed by police responding to the attack. What ethics concerns would surround such a potential acquisition?

4. You are the assistant director of a museum and will attend an auction to bid on an object for the collection. You and the director (your boss, with whom you get along very well) have informally agreed upon a maximum cost for the purchase. At the auction, you and one other bidder are eventually the only two competing for the item. You take the liberty of bidding slightly beyond the agreed-upon level. You are successful. What, if any, ethical issues might there be as a result?

5. Your state has laws mandating archaeology surveys be conducted before any building can be done on certain sites deemed of possible historic or American Indian value. These digs must be conducted by qualified professionals and at the expense of the landowner. What is retrieved must be held in perpetuity by a designated museum or similar cultural agency or entity. Your museum is considering becoming one of these. The state underwrites the housing, collection management, and use of the retrieved material. What ethics issues might surround being a state-designated repository of this sort?

museums set for themselves requires that they have something to preserve. Myriad objects are thus acquired and saved as evidence of abstract concepts about designated ideas, memories, theories, beliefs, feelings, etc., whatever the higher calling is for a museum's mission. Museum collecting methods flow from acquisition ethics. The next chapter delves into these in detail as the specifics are critical to unencumbered collecting successes.

Notes

1. Thomas Hoving, *The Chase, the Capture: Collecting at the Metropolitan* (New York: The Metropolitan Museum of Art, 1975), 1.

2. Rachel Nuwer, "When the Poacher is a Scientist," *New York Times*, April 2, 2019, Science Times, D1.

3. Ibid., D1.

4. Ibid., D6.

5. Sir William Henry Flower, *Essays on Museums and Other Subjects Connected with Natural History* (London: Macmillan and Co., 1898), 57. Classic Reprints, quoting Professor Brown Goode, director of the United States National Museum.

6. Rebecca Buck and Jean Allman Gilman, *Museum Registration Methods*, 5th ed. (Washington, DC: The AAM Press, 2010).

6

ACQUISITION ETHICS

*When collections cease to grow they begin to decay. A finished museum
is a dead museum, and a dead museum is a useless museum.*[1]

As previously discussed, most museum acquisitions take
place because of positive and ethical museum collecting
methods. This chapter presents standard procedures and
options that should be addressed before something is added to a permanent collection. A wide range of concerns lurk throughout the processes. A
well-articulated collecting policy will define an ethos that results in narrow
and simple directives about what to bring into a museum. This does not
mean a plethora of objects fall outside a desirable spectrum. It just gives
more reasons to decline things. Inapplicable collections use valuable space,
time, and money and skew institutional missions. This chapter presents
sound as well as unsuitable collecting arguments. It also addresses new
collecting issues embroiling museums. The acquisition work of museums
is an ever-evolving pursuit with ever-evolving ethical consequences.

Collecting Qualifications Checklist

When deciding what to collect, museums usually prioritize approaches.
This is true for art, history, and science institutions. The first and most

important subject to confirm is mission relevancy. Is an object directly and explicitly about the museum's subject? Various people may be involved in assessing this. In the final analysis, pertinent staff should be the ones to make a recommendation to acquire an object. They will also be the people declining additions. Part of their assessment process will involve determining how an acquisition fits with existing museum collections. Objects can be unique to a museum or meld with collections. The condition of an object is essential to understand during a collecting process. Is it original, has it been heavily "restored," does it exist in its entirety or is it part of a larger object or collection? Will it need special care and attention either for storage or for conservation? Finally, is the acquisition feasible? The following checklist briefly explains these priorities. While arranged in process order, it can unfold in a less linear and often simultaneous manner.

1. Relevance

    Items sought by museums must adhere to an institution's mission. Objects should provide meaningful direct evidence about the museum's subject. They should never be peripheral or irrelevant to that purpose. The evidentiary role of museum collections is essential to having them—otherwise why collect?
2. Collecting staff

    Traditionally, museum staff curators are the primary people responsible for recommending, acquiring, and stewarding collections. While some things are acquired by others, curators are usually best prepared for this task. When an acquisition is being considered, collection managers, conservators, and specialists with knowledge about an object or its field may also be involved. Is it ethical to let nonmuseum employees make acquisition decisions? Usually no. Recently, a sort of crowd-sourcing collecting has unfolded in certain museums. Institutions have invited members of its community (however that is defined) to suggest acquisitions. This is a tiny development in the field, but one worth noting in the context of the ethics of collecting. On the surface it may seem wise and innocuous but over the long term "it can bring in too many things if it's too easy, or too few things, if it's challenging, or the wrong things, if direction is unclear."[2] Things may come in that are of little intellectual value going forward. Exercising knowledgeable curatorial control can be offensive to nonmuseum staff participants, but if done with sensitivity, it can work and ward against future possession problems.

3. Relationship with existing museum collections

Museum collections do not exist in a vacuum. A painting, a fossil, a chair, a textile, a vase, can relate to similar objects in scholarly and/or visual ways. Some do so more than others, of course. When an item is proposed for a museum collection, where will it fit in with the overall collection of its type, time period, phylum, material, etc.? Ethics are hardly removed from these discussions. Will something be unique or duplicative and does that matter? Will it improve an aspect of a museum's holdings or reduce the quality, however that is defined? Is it more ethical to add to collection strengths or improve collection weaknesses? Is it ethical to collect something of lesser quality just because it is available? Also, will the considered acquisition pose a danger to existing collections, personnel, or the museum? This might be the case with munitions, toxic substances, or insect-infested items.

4. Condition

The physical condition of museum collections is of immense consequence. As preservation organizations, retaining objects in a sound state for present and future use is paramount. Much effort is devoted to this responsibility. When thinking about acquiring an object, it is of great importance to know how physically stable it is, how much of it is original to when it was created, and if the museum can adequately care for it. Arguments have been offered that it is unethical to accept objects that are in such poor condition as to threaten their continued existence or things around which they might be held. Museums need to know and support the material state of their collections.

5. Feasibility

Collecting in an ethical fashion usually means following codified professional standards. These are well explained in collection management publications.[3] Presumably museums will not acquire objects for which they cannot provide adequate documentary oversight, physical care, and intellectual access and use. It is unethical to do so.

Ethically Valid and Questionable Arguments for an Acquisition

Whether an object is donated, purchased, or field collected, acquisition arguments hold decisive implications. On the surface, it might seem that art, history, and science museums collect quite differently. Actually, they

ETHICAL AND QUESTIONABLE ACQUISITION ARGUMENTS

ETHICAL ACQUISITION ARGUMENTS

- This item is ideally suited to the mission of our museum and we can preserve and use it responsibly.
- We have been looking for such an object for years.
- We had no idea the item existed, and its obvious relevance will make it a great new addition to our holdings.
- The piece(s) signals an exciting unanticipated but relevant expansion of our mission that we can celebrate and sustain.

QUESTIONABLE ACQUISITION ARGUMENTS

- The object was left anonymously at the admission desk, so we figured we had to keep it.
- The donor is a board member.
- A trustee likes it.
- The public will like it.
- The item is worth a lot of money.
- The donor is so nice and has been such a loyal supporter of the museum we could not say no.
- It may have nothing to do with our mission, but it relates to other items that also have nothing to do with our mission.
- The donor is capable of helping the museum in very substantial ways.
- We can sell it later for something we really want.
- The donation is huge (in number or object size).
- It will make us famous.
- The object is kind of what we might like to have.
- We were given money to buy it.
- To get it we have to guarantee it will be on permanent exhibit.
- It doesn't fit our mission, but it came along with things that do and we had to take the whole group.
- It is irrelevant but we found it in storage and thought we should accession it anyway.

share similar approaches. As noted above, each institution must have legal and preferably unrestricted ownership; an object's condition must be secure; the museum needs to have the ability to care for an item now and presumably in the future; an item should fit with existing collections and pose no hazards to people, the museum, or other collections. Finally, all museums need to confirm what inherent preservation imperative exists to cause an item to be an acquisition priority.

Museums that set and abide by logical and disciplined collecting guidelines and goals will avoid being overwhelmed by superfluous things that cost money, take up precious space, and needlessly occupy staff attention.

Collecting Ethics Issues Embroiling Museums

When museums grapple with the fallout of questionable acquisition behavior, corrective measures must be taken. In addition to the aforementioned ethics questions posed within museums, parties outside them and the media in particular have embroiled museums in at least nine areas of investigation. Ordinary journalists as well as those with specific interests in various culture realms report on these with alarming frequency.

1. *Questions about the legitimacy of any sale or gift to a museum by individuals who may or may not have had the right to do so will expand.*

   Asking who has the right to sell or give something to a museum covers several collecting areas already. As discussed, these include art stolen or acquired by the Nazis through forced sales. Things of importance to residents of places once colonized by European nations and taken by the colonizers may be in museum collections now. Heirs to an estate could challenge either a will or the decisions of executors. An individual may say an object donor or seller had no right to do that. Simply questioning a sale or donation does not mean the accusation is illegitimate. An accused museum has a legal obligation to defend ownership. These questions are always couched in ethics terms.

2. *Controversies will escalate regarding how human remains are collected and used by museums.*

   Human remains of any sort are an increasingly sensitive subject for museums. Ethics is always the dominant argument regarding the ownership and use of these collections. Archaeology museums have been in the forefront of establishing protocols and guidelines. The collections of the museum at the University of Pennsylvania are the result of many excavations, principally in the Middle East. The museum has an exemplary public statement regarding how it deals with human remains both with existing and new collections (appendix IV).

3. *Demands for either the return or respectful handling of art and spiritually valued artifacts will increase.*

Though initially addressed in the United States by the Native American Graves Protection and Repatriation Act passed by Congress in 1990, the global scope of this issue is expanding in spirit and application if not by law. In addition to the sensitive nature of human remains, controversy can surround how objects of spiritual or broader cultural significance are collected and used by museums. Again, arguments about (usually against) museum ownership and use are always based on who has the ethical standing to support an accusation.

As the time of this writing, an interesting legal case focused on two daguerreotype photographs owned by Harvard University's Peabody Museum of Archaeology and Ethnography. The daguerreotypes were taken in 1850 in South Carolina and show individual enslaved people facing the camera, nude from the waste up. One is a female, named Delia, and one is a male, named Renty. The photographs were among several taken at the request of Louis Agassiz, who was a famous biologist at Harvard. He argued that people of African descent were inferior to other races. A family from Connecticut claims Renty as an ancestor and wants the photographs given to them. They have no legal claim to the images but base their demand on ethical considerations stating that the photographs were stolen from his ancestors who had no say in their making or use.[4]

4. *Issues about art, artifacts, or scientific specimens lost by private or institutional owners during war and civic disturbance will grow.*

Since World War II, much attention has focused on art stolen or taken through forced sales by the Nazis before and during the war. The problem has expanded to include similar circumstances as a result of other conflicts and civil disruptions. While on the surface it would appear that original owners or legitimate heirs have ethically sound arguments for restitution, there are differences of opinion. These differences are increasing. Responding to ownership debates will keep lawyers, politicians, government officials, and special interest groups occupied for years. Fraudulent documentation and spurious provenance declarations are common. A recent case found in favor of heirs claiming ownership of two drawings by the acclaimed Austrian artist Egon Schiele. It was noted that the supposed documentation supporting the legitimacy of their purchase after World War II was not "treated . . . as substantial evidence."[5]

Art plundered from museums in Middle Eastern countries during recent wars in that region frequently appear on the antiquities market. Museums must be cautious when considering the acquisition of such materials. Sellers are rarely concerned with the ethics of their commerce. Museums are learning to be more skeptical than once was the case. That protective stance should include alerting trusted authorities about sale offers of a suspicious nature.

5. *Museums need to be more mindful about collecting that threatens endangered species.*

   Museum acquisitions made of elements taken from endangered or threatened animal species or those animals in whole either need to be avoided or done in accord with whatever official permissions are required and supportive for collecting. Ivory is of special concern now, and it need not be newly poached. Old ivory carvings or hunting trophies are subject to impoundment by authorities in several nations. Natural history museums may seem the most affected by these concerns, but decorative arts objects found in history and art museums can be included if they hold ivory. Certain bird feathers and the skin of protected species are similarly subject to legal protections.

6. *Acquisitions must not be a danger to themselves, museum staff, or the public.*

   A collecting ethics concern includes items with inherent hazardous materials. Natural history specimens can be especially problematic. Old taxidermy mounts were often made using asbestos, lead, mercury, and arsenic. There is a reason they can look pristine, or at least not infested. Bugs have avoided them. Vermin can, however, be present in items being accessioned, and this must obviously be avoided. Animal specimens and human organs preserved in liquid and held in jars or other sealed containers require care when accessioning. Art museum employees need to know what materials an artist used in paintings, sculptures, graphics, etc. A vast array of materials can be found in all sorts of contemporary art. History museums should be careful with armaments. It is unethical for museum leaders and personnel to ignore collection-based hazards.

7. *Museums must watch for possible failures to abide by perceived or actual donation expectations.*

Soon, or even long after something is given to a museum, a donor may decide the institution has not lived up to its promise (documented or assumed) to care for and use the object in ways originally envisioned at the time of the gift. This can be a cause of, or response to, deaccessioning. Donors of some gifts to museums may question how an institution is treating the items given. If either implied or agreed-upon care and use is unsatisfactory, complaints may be lodged. Either requests are made for the return of objects or changes must be made to their institutional stewardship. New legal disputes can erupt regarding perceived contradictions of a museum's purpose.[6]

8. *There are surging demands internationally for the return of property of cultural significance to a people and place of origin.*

There is a rising tide of requests from countries in sub-Saharan Africa, Central and South America, and the lower Pacific Rim in particular for museums in Europe and the United States to return objects of cultural value that were taken by force, deception, under adverse circumstances, or by concocted sale conditions from the original native owners. The removals were done variously by military occupiers, explorers, natural scientists, missionaries, collectors, or treasure hunters. Now called restitution or repatriation, the collection shifting involves transferring museum objects to countries or people claiming origin ownership and undue historic loss. The objects were presumably made or used by ancestors of the requesting peoples or are of other significant cultural value. The uproar is totally based on arguments that the museum has no ethical right to own whatever is being sought for a return.

In 2002, eighteen large museums signed a public statement briefly extolling the virtues of museums holding collections reflecting world cultures (appendix II). The Declaration on the Importance and Value of Universal Museums has been highly criticized by nonparticipants. The debate has caused supporters of universal museums to request considerations when object return is a possibility. They ask that existing laws be abided by, not ones that people might hope to exist. They want people to recognize the intellectual losses that can accrue with unfettered collection removals, especially if such removals would mean the total absence of materials about a subject of immense importance to the museum. It is hoped there will be assurances for the proper conservation of whatever object is being considered for removal from a museum. People should be mindful of the value of keeping museum collections in the public sector regardless of what country they may be transferred to. Everyone must remember that geopolitical entities requesting the "return" of an item may not have existed when it was made, used, or obtained by a museum. Finally, negotiators should consider cultural exchanges or shared ownership arrangements that would benefit the museum from which an object is leaving, the new location of the object, and its scholarly value.[7]

9. *Ethical relations with living artists or artist estates will continue to be highly sensitive and conflicts will escalate.*

Art museums have long worked with living artists or their heirs and estates. For the most part, these relationships have been successful. However, there have been problems. With the increase in artist-rights organizations, the growing field of "art law," and attorneys who specialize in legal matters relating to visual productions, complications can arise that not only give museums bad publicity but cost them time and money.

Museum Responses to Collecting Ethics Accusations

When museums are accused of unethical or illegal collection ownership, depending on the circumstances, responses will include:

- We took the item in question in good faith and there is no evidence to the contrary.
- At the time of its acquisition by us, we held undisputed, signed documented ownership. That circumstance is only now being questioned.
- It was acquired many years ago and who knows where it actually originated before it found its way to our museum.
- At the time of acquisition, we received it with the full permission and knowledge of the person(s) or governing authority of the place it came from.
- Do those demanding a return of something have the right to do so and how is that determined?

- The country demanding the return has an unstable government and is notoriously corrupt.
- Why should we return something to a country that has a terrible record of preserving its own patrimony or is clearly incapable of doing so now?
- How can we be certain the case against our ownership of a piece has merit?
- The artist gave us her work with no restrictions and included our right to reproduce it in any manner we wished.
- The country claiming ownership of a piece did not exist when the piece was removed from the place that is now part of the claimant country.
- The museum should be thanked for preserving an important object that would surely have not survived given the original use of the item or turmoil that has afflicted the place it came from over the years.
- The object is only important because it is in a museum; otherwise, no one would show any interest it.
- The object has been in our possession for decades and no one has previously contested our ownership. Our possession has been public knowledge.

Miscellaneous

Is it ethical for a museum to agree to a collection donor's gift caveats in spite of customary advice against the practice? Clearly it depends on the donor, the collection, the caveats, and the particular museum being courted or doing the courting. A restriction that might seem ethically acceptable was agreed to when the Vermont Historical Society, in Barre, was given the state prison's last electric chair. The transfer forbids exhibiting the chair. In storage, it is covered to avoid disturbing staff, scholars, or visitors to the otherwise restricted facility. The value of the object historically is not disputed, and it may be the only item of its kind in any museum. In this case, preservation rather than display is the obvious collecting argument.[8]

A more prominent public example of a collection donation restriction is seen in the Robert Lehman Wing at the Metropolitan Museum of Art (figure 6.1). This large addition to the museum's encyclopedic sprawl was the gift of its namesake, Robert Lehman (1891–1969). He was a scion of the Lehman family financial businesses. Among his several personal interests was collecting art, largely of the Renaissance. At one point during his life, it was arguably the most important private collection of its kind. The museum was delighted to acquire it by meeting the donor's exacting demands. The art was to be contained in its own, new, wing and shown as if in his New York City townhouse. The gift was not without controversy. Some people questioned the ethics of creating what they saw as a personal shrine that contradicts the museum's chronological, geographical, and content arranged galleries.[9]

Figure 6.1. The Robert Lehman Collection Wing of the Metropolitan Museum of Art. Photo by Steven Miller © 2019

Museums that acquire contemporary art must always be mindful of ethics related to the artists whose work is collected and the role of donors. One of the most impressive accolades artists can enjoy is to be in a museum collection. In the past, it was fairly common for curators of new art to personally own art by the artists they collected for the museum they worked in. The camaraderie artists and curators enjoyed was one of mutual respect, support, and admiration. I know a retired curator who was with a major American art museum for many years. At the beginning of his career, he worked for a leading commercial gallery. His Manhattan loft is full of art by artists who gave him work solely out of friendship. He has never sold anything. No artist received an exhibit in exchange for a personal gift.

Times have evolved as far as museum ethics related to personal collecting by employees is concerned. It is generally considered unethical for staff to collect what the museum employing them collects. Personnel manuals usually contain directives about this. Of course, there will be exceptions. If a new hire happens to already own things of the sort the museum employing him or her has, this will presumably be known during the interview process. An accommodation will be reached whereby personal collecting or selling of such items will be suspended or will proceed only with museum preapproval.

The ethics of a museum acquiring the kind of art a trustee collects can cause problems or at least raise a few eyebrows. Good museum trustees are hard to find. This is especially true when an institution is looking for people who can contribute wisdom, wealth, and work in their volunteer capacities. It is not unusual for a few great trustees to share the same collecting passions as the organization they serve. Historically, this sort of overlap was accepted as welcome evidence of shared passions. Today, it is either ignored, warned against in documents relating to volunteers (which trustees are), or noted in the annual conflict-of-interest forms trustees file with the museums they serve.

In Summary

Most museum collections are and will continue to be sought in appropriate and ethical ways. Process guidelines and caveats are well understood. Stumbles are exceptions. Most collecting policies should include content to address problems. Corrective action can be taken. The results must

1. How can a museum know a collection donor has the legal right to do so and what ethics need to be considered while assuring this outcome?

2. You are a curator at a New York City history museum. One day you get a call from the security guard at the admission desk. A man is demanding to take away an object on temporary exhibit in the grand entry hall. He claims the lender is not the rightful owner. You do not give him the item. He proceeds to sue the lender and loses the first court case. He wins on appeal. The museum had planned to purchase the artifact from the original lender but now makes the same offer to the actual and legal owner. He accepts. While the proceedings unfolded, courts agreed the museum could hold the piece as it was the ideal safe haven. What ethics issues need to be understood, investigated, abided by, etc. in this situation?

3. You are the director of a historic tavern museum in a major East Coast city. You are also the curator, a job for which you are highly qualified. You have been there six years and never received complaints about your work. The house is furnished with antiques representing its Revolutionary War interpretive period. None are original to the site. All were acquired by gift over the past ninety years. Acquisition records are in order and everything is accessioned and catalogued both in hard copy and in a collection management database. The museum has long had a collection committee of the board, which approved all past acquisitions.

   A member of the museum's board of trustees is moving from a large house outside the city to a small apartment in the city. He collects domestic antiques of the same period as your museum. He wants to give the museum much of his furniture and have the museum sell what it already has. You, as curator, are opposed to this and have explained your position to the trustee and the full board, including the collection committee. The trustee has expressed his displeasure with you in vitriolic email and hard copy memo attacks condemning your qualifications and work. What ethical issues are involved in this situation?

4. A woman calls your museum to say her father was mentally incapacitated when he donated an object to its collection forty years ago. She wants it. The museum has an excellent collection management office and has since its start a hundred years ago. The acquisition documentation for the object appears valid and includes signed gift forms. How should the museum respond to this request and what, if any, ethical concerns might there be in handling the situation?

benefit the long-term sustenance of what an institution actually needs and wants. Regular reviews of existing acquisition policies are essential—especially in light of new and often unanticipated controversies that will surely crop up.

Defining with specificity what a museum should collect, and how, is of fundamental importance. It is estimated that the vast majority of things museums are offered, by either sale or gift, are rejected. This development is to be applauded and emulated going forward. Declining possible acquisitions can be done in a polite and informative way. When museums do acquire an object, vigilance from a documentation perspective is essential. Accurate, honest, complete, safely retained, and easy-to-understand records not only help protect a museum should debates erupt, but they play an authentication and provenance role. The subject of collection veracity is discussed in the following chapter. Museums work hard to assure the honesty of what they have. Indeed, this is a core definition of why they exist.

Notes

1. Sir William Henry Flower, *Essays on Museums and Other Subjects Connected with Natural History* (London: Macmillan and Co., 1898), 57. Classic Reprints, quoting Professor Brown Goode, director of the United States National Museum.

2. Steven Lubar, *Inside the Lost Museum: Curating, Past and Present* (Cambridge, MA: Harvard University Press, 2017), 91.

3. See, for example, Rebecca Buck and Jean Allman Gilman, *Museum Registration Methods*, 5th ed. (Washington, DC: The AAM Press, 2010), 36.

4. Jennifer Schuessler, "Portraits of Slaves Require Moral Lens," *New York Times*, March 23, 2019, C4.

5. William D. Cohan, "Court Says Victim's Heirs Can Keep Returned Art," *New York Times*, July 11, 2019, C3.

6. Robin Scher, "Better Safe Than Sorry: With the Repatriation of African Art Making Headlines in Europe, American Museums are Taking Preemptive Measures," *ARTNews*, Summer 2019, 86–91.

7. Adrian Ellis, "Restitution to Africa Reaches Tipping Point," *The Art Newspaper*, #331, April 2019, 14.

8. John Lippman, "Vermont Historical Society Stores Windsor State Prison's Electric Chair," *Valley News*, August 7, 2017, https://www.vnews.com/Vermont-s-electric-chair-hidden-in-Barre-11676974.

9. Ada Louise Huxtable, "Architecture View. 'Wrong but Impeccable,'" *New York Times*, May 25, 1975, 109, https://www.nytimes.com/1975/05/25/archives/architecture-view-wrong-but-impeccable-architecture-view.html.

7

ETHICS AND COLLECTION AUTHENTICITY

He who knows a thousand works of art, knows a thousand frauds.[1]

Museums purport to be places of truth. Objects are the devices used to meet this objective. Ultimately, they play one role—to exist as proof of a subject. In that capacity they must be associated directly with whatever topic is discussed in an exhibition, publication, research project, etc. This chapter examines intellectual and practical forces surrounding collection honesty from varying ethical perspectives.

Collection Honesty

Museums are forums for communicating about history, art, and science. With their collections and associated programming, museums connect past and present generations. The assumption is this will continue for future generations. Essentially, museums use the tangible to explain, discuss, examine, celebrate, ponder, explore, and analyze the intangible. The role of museum collections as fact-messengers infects objects with a host of ethical conundrums. At the top of the list is authenticity.

Are the things we see in museums actually what those institutions say they are? Museums devote inordinate resources to assuring collection honesty. How that is defined depends on the museum, its mission, and what it decides to collect. A history museum may want a certain automobile because a famous person owned it. A science museum could want that same automobile because of its engineering. An art museum shows the car for its design. In any of these cases, the vehicle in question will usually not be a reproduction, facsimile, or badly "restored" version of the original. While these can be found in museums, they should be labeled as such and serve as exhibition props rather than documentary proof.

The idea of objects being used as evidence to make a point is nothing new and in fact does not originate with museums. It has been going on for thousands of years if archaeological findings and ancient art is to be believed. Religious reliquaries, too, provide an illustrative analogy. Indeed, museums are heirs to these. Presenting the alleged bones of a saint, hairs of a sacred personage, or clothing worn by a venerated spiritual luminary forecast museum collecting and exhibiting. From a content perspective, the difference between relics and museums is honesty. Except for some true believers, what the former items claim to be may or may not be true. Most of what museums hold is what they say it is, at least in objective, fair-minded democratic institutions operating in free societies.

For collections to be most effective and maximize their ethical character, they must be original to, for, or about the subject of an institution's mission. In this context, "original" equates with authentic. Museum collections are three-dimensional documents. Objects provide testimony to truths decided upon by museum founders, employees, and supporters. Museums are odd among human inventions in their unbridled reliance on physical stuff as primary source materials for knowledge of the human and natural universe. I am fond of saying the only thing that makes museums unique is the real thing.

How museums assure the authenticity of their collections starts with their founding. The new National Museum of African American History and Culture in Washington, DC, offers an excellent example. A group of people decided there was a need for the museum. There were many reasons for the idea. Foremost was a concern that the subject of African American history in the United States deserved prominent attention, and in Washington, DC. To establish the museum, a top priority was to form a permanent collection. No one goes to an empty museum.

An impressive national effort was made to seek a wide range of original material evidence about the African American experience. Objects were needed to prove positive and negative realities of this history, whether they reflected the ordinary or the extraordinary. "The museum's team collected artifacts from around the nation in an 'Antiques Road-show'–style program in 15 cities called 'Save Our African American Treasures.' The program yielded many of the 40,000 objects the museum now holds."[2]

Affirming collection authenticity begins when something is being acquired. For art museums, it can center on knowing a painting is by a particular artist and it is in a medium that makes sense for the artist working at the time the picture was made. Rembrandt did not paint with acrylics. History museums strive to guarantee the authenticity of their collections. When we see the Bible owned by the corrupt mid-nineteenth-century convicted New York City political scallywag "Boss Tweed" at the Museum of the City of New York, we can rest assured it is just that. We are free to make whatever assumptions we wish about the man.

The role of the original object justifying a museum's value is perhaps best illustrated by the National Air and Space Museum in Washington, DC. It is the most popular museum in the United States. Why? The history of flight is spread before visitors immediately upon entering. From the first successful motorized airplane (the Wright brothers' airplane) to space flight, the array of collections presented is impressive and easily grasped. And everything you see is the real thing.

History and art museums are not the only institutions that need to be careful regarding object authenticity. Science museums can run afoul of fakes, especially when it comes to dinosaur fossils. This began at least two centuries ago when a growing commercial market caused "some hucksters to combine different fossils into a more impressive assemblage" that increased the fake creature's market value. "Such frauds were notoriously difficult to spot." With a current marked increase in private individual desires for fossils, the market "has roared back to life—and the old problem of fraud has returned to it." "A number of seemingly groundbreaking discoveries have turned out to be artifacts of commercial deceit."[3]

The unique object-centric purpose of museums infuses them all regardless of size, location, or subject matter. The work to guarantee content validity is paramount. It is an ongoing duty. As explained, museum employees responsible for collections are regular monitors of new and existing acquisitions insofar as their authenticity is concerned. How well they accomplish this can be seen in how they deal with authentication questions that occasionally arise.

Collection Veracity Snafus

When museums fail to meet their institutionally self-imposed ethical commitment to collection truth and know it, they need to acknowledge this for the record and in some public way. How this is done ethically can lead to debates. Should mistakes be kept quiet? What about changes in theories that result in different interpretations of collections—How should that be handled? Do museums need to be mindful of potential legal problems if the names of people responsible for a failed fact are made public? If fakes or questionable items are discovered in a museum collection, should they be retained, destroyed, sold in the gift shop, internally, or deaccessioned and turned over to educators to use as they wish?

There are several instances illustrating how museums have communicated failures or changes in the authenticity of collections. In the last century, the Metropolitan Museum of Art provided two good examples. Both involved sculptures. One was a group of three larger-than-life standing ceramic figures. The other was a cast bronze horse.

The ceramic pieces were purported to show ancient Etruscan warriors. They were purchased by the Met in the early twentieth century. While questions of authenticity were expressed by various scholars at the time, it was not until scientific testing found a material inconsistent with that used by ancient ceramicists in Italy. Certain physical anomalies became apparent, also. In 1961, the Met announced the figures were fakes. They remain in the museum's collection but are not on view. For scholarly reasons and to guard against potential illicit commercial market involvement, the museum retains items deemed fraudulent that are discovered in its holdings. After the museum acted on its suspicions, the Italian forgers confessed.

The saga of the bronze horse is more complex. When purchased from a dealer in Paris in 1923, it was thought to be Greek, dating from the Early Classical period of the fifth century BC. In the late 1960s, an administrator at the museum decided it was a fake (figure 7.1). His

Figure 7.1. Classical Bronze Horse, Metropolitan Museum of Art. Photo by Steven Miller © 2018

opinion was based on his amateur interest in ancient sculpture and ceramics, flawed visual observations, and a negligible scientific test. The museum announced this discovery at a series of seminars on art forgery presented in November and December 1967. These were published in its February 1968 bulletin.[4]

In 1972, the museum reversed its opinion of the horse's antiquity. A conservation cleaning had removed misleading surface accretions from when it had been cast for reproductions sold in the gift shop. The administrator had mistaken these for evidence of how the horse was made. He thought it was done by a method unknown to the ancient sculpture technicians. By this time, he had left the museum to direct another, but he rescinded his original pronouncement. The new information suggested the horse was still Greek but dated to the late Hellenist period.[5]

After the Metropolitan Museum of Art decided the ancient bronze horse was not a fake, it presented a temporary exhibition explaining the history of the sculpture. The information told of its acquisition and the 1960s scholarly debate about its originality. This was possibly a public relations "first" for a museum. While institutions might admit acquisition errors, presenting the deliberations that unfolded over the topic is unusual to say the least. Presumably, the museum felt ethically compelled to clear the air as the piece in question was found to be historically sound. It is one thing to have incorrect evidence in a collection, but it is quite another to brand something false when that is wrong. As the famous art historian Max Friedländer stated: "It is indeed an error to collect a forgery, but it is a sin to stamp a genuine piece with the seal of falsehood."[6]

In 2017, a revelation about phony items in a museum's collections was announced by the Mexican Museum in San Francisco. A study found that "only 83 of the 2,000 artifacts in the museum's pre-Hispanic or pre-Columbian era collection could be authenticated. . . . The other 1,917 are considered decorative and will probably be donated to schools or smaller museums."[7]

The three public corrective amplifications cited above address exceptional situations. The authenticity of most museum collections is rarely in doubt because of the initial acquisition rigor shown by those responsible for museum collecting. One charge is to avoid fakes, forgeries, reproductions, facsimiles, or the bogus in collections unless they have direct and immediate relevance to a museum's topic.

Collection Scholarship Ethics

Museum scholarship must be done for sound, ethical reasons. It cannot be a game pursued to meet egotistical trustees or staff desires to pump up their status. Pretending an item is something it is not, just to advance a career, promote an institution's reputation, or cover up a mistake contradicts the truth foundations upon which museums are built. How museums parse collection truth depends on the museum and what it owns. A twentieth-century historic house museum might have a dining room full of reproduction Chippendale-style furniture, but those chairs, tables, and sideboards are not being jettisoned because they were made in the 1900s rather than the 1800s. They are retained because they were used in the house by the owners whose residency is interpreted as part of the history of the home. They are original to that time rather than when the style was created.

The role of collections in historic structures, homes in particular, is discussed elsewhere in this text. It must be referred to regarding museum collection authenticity and the ethics thereof. The furnishings in Olana, the Catskill, New York, home built and occupied by the famous Hudson River School painter Frederic Edwin Church (1826–1900), are all original to the house. They thus offer proof of his residency and interior design tastes, and capture a unique time and place in wealthy American domestic life.

The Half-Moon Inn, owned by the Newtown Historic Association in Newtown, Pennsylvania, is furnished conjecturally as might have been the case in its mid-eighteenth-century time of origin. The collections shown were largely purchased or donated in the 1960s when the building was being converted into a museum. Tours of the site explain this. The interpretive ethics regarding the collections are sound.

Thomas Hoving (1931–2009) fancied himself a fake-buster and indeed spent much of his life talking about that after being director of the Metropolitan Museum of Art in New York City. Considering his love of hucksterism and reputation for self-aggrandizement, people were never too sure of his credentials in this regard. The scope of things he purported to fake-bust was vast, but in the abstract, his points were valid and the emphasis on museum avoidance of the phony was the ethical thing to do.

In my experience, museums do their very best to avoid fakes and for the most part they succeed. Museum authenticity ethically adheres to collecting standards people have come to expect. Whenever surveys are done regarding the veracity of museums, respondents hold them in high esteem. Visitors believe what they see, read, and hear in galleries. This trust originates from the objects on view as well as the verbal materials interpreting them. There are sound academic reasons for this. Though most museum visitors are hardly experts on any of the vast collections held on their behalf, they have learned to believe what a responsible museum tells them in the exhibition context or through other information presented. They believe museums tell the truth.[8]

1. You are the curator of an automobile museum in Ohio. A famous race-car driver offers to give the museum the car he raced to victory recently at a nearby track in an important national competition. He has raced the car for the past few years. No cars of its type, age, or ownership status are represented in the collection. You (on behalf of the museum and with the board of trustees' approval) agree to the donation. When the car is delivered by the owner, he has had it repainted, new decals have been applied, and it no longer appears as it did in the recent race, or even before that. He wanted it to look its best for the museum. What, if any, veracity ethics issues does this present the museum?

2. You are curating an exhibit of photographs by a deceased photographer. The pictures on view are being made from original negatives by a commercial photo reproduction service. A few "vintage" prints will be included. These were made by the photographer in her darkroom. Are there ethical issues to be explained or addressed in the exhibition because of this content decision?

3. The staff responsible for keeping the historic house museum you direct clean is part of the buildings and grounds department. They are referred to as "housekeepers." In the course of their work, they vacuum floors, curtains, and draperies, as well as dust, clean windows, and polish wood surfaces. They have no training or background in museum conservation. They have never received instructions about how to do their work, when, with what materials, etc. What ethics concerns should the museum have in this regard?

4. As an amateur dinosaur buff your research has determined that the head attached to a dinosaur skeleton on exhibit in the natural history museum is incorrect for the particular species. You manage the museum's sales shop. In the nineteenth century, when this item was acquired by the museum, such mismatching of fossils was a common occurrence as museums were furiously competing to show dramatic examples of these long-extinct creatures. The practice continues, especially with freelance excavators who make a living finding, rearranging, and selling bones on the open market. From an ethics perspective, what should you do with this information?

When we use the word "truth," we can be on a very slippery slope. What is the truth, whose truth is it, how is it determined? Is truth fungible, temporary, or forever? Is it singular or plural, is there one truth or are there multiple truths? This is not the place for a long philosophical discourse on the nature of truth, but it is the central concern regarding how museums act when it comes to collections. Physical evidence substantiates museum missions. Objects "hold truths." "Historians and archeologists have worked hard to use objects as evidence."[9] "Artifacts in a museum carry with them the power of authenticity." "In part that is because museums have real things."[10] Matters of truth and ethics are inextricably linked for museums.

In Summary

We understand the essential role ethics plays in authenticating museum collections. The honesty of a museum object extends beyond the thing itself. It includes some or all of the scholarship that surrounds it. Errors in collection veracity take place purposely or innocently. Certainly there is a long tradition of faking the sorts of things museums collect, be it art, historic artifacts, or scientific specimens. Every museum of any age and stature has had to deal with questionable collection situations. The correct response is to accept this reality head-on and correct evidence and errors.

Owning valued objects for long-term public benefit requires not only that they be what museums say they are, but that they are collected for worthy applications. How that is arranged is the topic of the following chapter. It is essential for outcome-based reasons to assure museums are more than morgues holding art, artifacts, and scientific specimens secretly and privately. Accessing and using collections is of increasing importance from ethical, practical, intellectual, and financial perspectives.

Notes

1. Horace, as quoted by Thomas Hoving, *False Impressions: The Hunt for Big-Time Art Fakes* (New York: Simon and Schuster, 1996), preface.
2. Graham Bowley, "How the Fight for a National African-American Museum Was Won," *New York Times*, September 5, 2016, https://www.nytimes.com/2016/09/05/arts/design/how-the-fight-for-a-national-african-american-museum-was-won.html?_r=0.

3. Lukas Rieppel, "The Problem With Buying Dinosaurs," *Wall Street Journal*, June 22, 2019, C3.

4. "Art Forgery," special issue, *The Metropolitan Museum of Art Bulletin*, 26, no. 6 (February 1968).

5. David L. Shirey, "Metropolitan Bronze Horse Proves to Be Ancient," *New York Times*, December 24, 1972, https://www.nytimes.com/1972/12/24/archives/metropolitan-bronze-horse-proves-to-be-ancient.html.

6. Max Friedlander, as quoted by Thomas P. F. Hoving, "The Game of Duplicity," in "Art Forgery," special issue, *The Metropolitan Museum of Art Bulletin*, 26, no. 6 (February 1968), 241.

7. Associated Press, "Most of Oldest Items in San Francisco's Mexican Museum Aren't the Real Deal," *Los Angeles Times*, July 7, 2017, https://www.latimes.com/local/lanow/la-me-museum-fakes-20170707-story.html.

8. "In Museums We Trust. Here's How Much (Data Update), Colleendilenschneider, March 6, 2019, https://www.colleendilen.com/2019/03/06/in-museums-we-trust-heres-how-much-data-update/.

9. Steven Lubar, *Inside the Lost Museum: Curating, Past and Present* (Cambridge, MA: Harvard University Press, 2017), 280.

10. Ibid., 164.

COLLECTION STEWARDSHIP AND ACCESS

Museums that neither care for their collections nor make them available are not really museums, only temporary rest homes for misplaced objects.[1]

Museum collection stewardship is the safe care and handling of an institution's accessioned objects. Access deals with how collections are used. This chapter discusses these twin duties and their ethics ramifications. They are more intertwined now than ever.

Stewardship

Stewardship begins when an item is being acquired. During the process, detailed and accurate documentation must be recorded. This typically involves assigning an item an accession number (which is unique to it) and establishing a paper and picture record of ownership, condition, and scholarly references. There are customary directives for how this should be done.[2] The information is usually retained in collection management files. Creating, retaining, and updating collection records are ethical priorities. Failing this duty in even the most rudimentary way is to miss a basic museum function.

Accessioned objects are placed in suitable storage facilities that are also largely under the supervision of collection managers. "When a museum takes an object into its permanent collections, it accessions the object and thereby makes a commitment to care for and conserve that object so that it can be used for research, exhibition, and education."[3]

Storage is a primary collection stewardship duty. Where and how something is kept will depend on the object. Automobiles will require different accommodations than postage stamps. Large outdoor sculpture narrows location options. Smaller sculpture can be moved about and be seen both inside and outside. Buildings that are considered collection objects tend to define where and how they can be kept. Storage needs to secure contents against theft, vandalism, and environmental depredations. Neglecting this responsibility is an obvious ethical breach.

Is prioritizing the sequence and extent of collection care determined by the size or magnitude of an acquisition; its condition; a monetary value; its content notoriety; the museum's exhibition needs; the nature of something's provenance; an emergency preservation need; a museum's budget capabilities? Or, do vacillating management preferences take effect in these decisions? The variable answer is yes. Any one or several of these factors can and will determine what sort of attention an item is given when acquired by a museum. Museums must be realists when it comes to collection care. Meeting high ethical standards is a laudable goal but paying for them can be a problem.

Long-term collection care means setting a policy written by qualified staff and approved by the museum's governing body. The actions should be recorded in meeting minutes and a copy of the document kept with those minutes. Remember, whatever is decided upon can be changed later. If so, that has to happen in a similar, authoritative recorded manner. As with all governing documents for a museum, ones for collection care commitment should be reviewed every few years. Ethics regarding collection stewardship and access are not static. Dramatic changes can happen suddenly or incrementally.

Documentation

Museum collections should be documented according to accepted professional standards. Such documentation should include a full identification and description of each item, its associations, provenance, condition, treatment, and present location. Such data should be kept in a secure environment and be supported by retrieval systems providing access to the information by the museum personnel and other legitimate users.[4]

It is a gross ethical violation for museums to acquire things and then ignore documenting them in a recognized professional manner. A collection object without a paper trail is an orphan object. Failing to create files about identity, condition, and provenance is unwise, to say the least. Defining what cataloguing means is obviously essential for any museum. Registrars and collection managers have excellent guidelines for this work.[5] Curators and others involved in the exercise may be less rigorous and consistent in their approaches to cataloguing. This is not to say the information they provide is invalid, only that it may be inconsistent. Regardless of how cataloguing is defined, it is a time-consuming exercise.

Assuring legal ownership is obviously critical when collecting. This is necessary for things archaeologically or field-retrieved, purchased privately or commercially, or donated to a museum. Occasionally, even the most dutiful ownership assurances can be questioned by outside interests after the fact, even long after the fact. This happens infrequently. Yet the mere possibility of such an occurrence only reinforces the ethical wisdom of accurate, honest, complete documentation of the gift, purchase, and field-retrieval or excavation transaction at the time it takes place.

How collection documentation is made available is a subject of growing importance for museums. Today, it is possible to at least get an introduction to collection content and scope online. A researcher in New Zealand can learn about the contents of a museum in Iceland. Certainly, not all museum collections are documented for computer access, but the future is promising. Controlling ethics considerations about this form of use must be established by a museum well in advance of implementing a process.

Storage

Most museum collections are in storage. There are two reasons for this. First, few museums have adequate space to safely show everything they own. Second, to be preserved for future generations, certain types of collections should not be displayed in certain ways.

In the past, ethics and museum storage were hardly melded topics. Where and how collections are kept is of little interest to most people outside the field. Some in the profession share the same feeling. Given the essential importance of collection storage, this myopia needs to be addressed. It is ethically essential that valued art, historic artifacts, and scientific specimens be well housed and secure for the long term.[6]

Museum storage can be misunderstood. Why are so many things kept out of sight? The complaint rests on an assumption that museums only collect for exhibit purposes. This is logical. The public's experience with museums largely happens in their galleries. Moreover, collections are seen in books, videos, PowerPoint presentations, and online in a host of applications. It is difficult to disabuse people of a preconceived notion. Some will accuse museums of ethical malpractice for inexplicably hiding what they own.

When someone frets that museum collections are often in storage more than on exhibit, an analogy I find helpful is to describe these things as documents held for their informational content or visual value. As such, they are akin to books in a library, most of which are not being read. In addition, light-sensitive materials such as photographs, textiles, and art on paper constitute a huge area of museum collecting. It would be expensive to try and exhibit these even on a rotating basis. They would also deteriorate. How ethical are these options?

Cumulatively, the vast majority of natural history museum collections are in storage. They exist as specimens carefully acquired over the years and held in drawers, in jars, on racks and shelves, and in other facility arrangements. "In the United States, natural history collections contain an estimated one billion specimens."[7] They constitute "a library filled with rare and important books."[8] "For some species, the few specimens placed in natural history collections worldwide are the only examples that exist: living specimens are gone."[9]

In his history of the American Museum of Natural History, author and former employee Douglas Preston wrote about its tens of millions of specimens. "Far from being a gigantic attic of seldom-seen curiosities, these collections are the lifeblood of the research that is being done at the Museum and, indeed, in the worldwide scientific community."[10] How critical is all the static material that is not on exhibit in natural history museums, not to mention art and history museums? Very. It would be so egregiously unethical to dispose of it. Fortunately, that almost never happens or is even suggested.

A new collection storage issue is part of a larger ethics concern expressed by peoples connected emotionally, culturally, historically, racially, ethnically, religiously, or personally to certain objects owned by museums. This has opened a wider realm of moral sensitivities. Certain items may have to be handled only by designated representatives of a particular group or peoples, or by individuals authorized by them to do so. It is possible these persons will not be museum employees. In addition, the objects may require specific storage arrangements. Previously, museums ignored original use sensitivities, or employees were completely unaware of original practices. With greatly enhanced diversity training and inclusion desires, new protocols and procedures are being learned on the job. This aspect of stewardship extends to more than storage when it comes to how particular collections are retained and accessed.[11]

As noted, on occasion museum collections in storage are potential safety threats. Science museums with natural history specimens originally placed in jars of hazardous liquids must be handled with care. Taxidermy mounts stuffed in past centuries can contain arsenic, lead, mercury, and asbestos. Protecting workers and the public from these toxic materials requires specific housing and handling guidelines. Guns and munitions need to be handled securely. Larger-scale potentially explosive armaments must be retained safely. The ethics of having and collecting potentially dangerous things must be discussed. Outcomes and approaches will depend on a particular museum. The first priority has to be protecting staff, the public, and the institution.

Climate control for collection storage can be a subject of ethics debate. Is it right to have and continue to acquire things when they will be kept in unsafe environments? If long-term preservation is a true goal of museums, various collections will need to be housed in ways that meet various environmental parameters. These usually include maintaining certain temperatures, humidity and light levels, and air quality controls. In some cases, damage resulting from vibrations must be addressed, as would be the case in galleries near highly trafficked roads or in earthquake prone areas. Museums located in flood-prone regions should be prepared for disaster. Climate change will see this increase.[12]

Use

Museums must be sensitive to the ethics of how collections are used. Exhibition applications have their own set of concerns, which are discussed in chapter 10. Collections are also used for research, promotional applications (as might be seen in advertisements), and in reproductions. At first, ethical concerns may seem negligible for these and related applications. However, there are a host of behavioral matters to be aware of, especially when it comes to objects that have a spiritual meaning for non-Western, non-European peoples.

Perhaps the most common way museum collections are used is by having them reproduced in some fashion. An analysis of this practice touches on the ethics of how objects are treated by museums. It is quite common for museums to provide reproductions of collection items. There is usually a charge for requests coming from outside an institution. Copies are made and used by people in many ways for many reasons. There are two reproduction choices: (1) providing images of collection objects and (2) making physical copies for decorative arts pieces such as furniture, ceramics, or glass objects, or for textile applications including scarves, jackets, and ties. Large museums will have departments devoted to reproduction services. Smaller organizations may allocate this work to individuals who are also responsible for other duties such as curating, collection management, directing, or operating a retail shop.

What ethical questions should museums ask when it comes to reproducing collections in the ways described above? There are several at least:

- Does the museum have the legal right to reproduce a particular collection object?
- What is the reproduction being used for? Does that correspond with a museum's mission and does that matter?
- Will the museum control how the reproduction is used along with its name?
- Who will do the copying?
- Can the museum protect against unauthorized use?
- Will the making of the copy endanger the original object in any way?
- Can the copying be made possible by the museum within its current work schedule and budget?

- If income is an outcome of the copying, is it a reasonable amount and how is "reasonable" defined?
- How do the costs compare to what other museums charge for the same services and does that matter?
- Who should have final reproduction authority for or at a museum?

The ethics of museum reproduction practices will vary according to individual and group opinion as well as a particular circumstance. Some might say no art should be reproduced in any manner whatsoever. People should only see paintings, prints, photographs, sculpture, etc. in the original. A related opinion argues that reproducing art piecemeal in ways the originals were never intended to be seen is an insult to the object and the artist (if known). Showing parts of Van Gogh's painting *Starry Night* (see figure 4.1) on an umbrella could be seen as an outrageous ethical affront to one of the most famous paintings in existence.[13]

For contemporary art, collection reproduction use will probably fall under current copyright laws. But museums use images in many ways. Even copyright laws may allow things with which artists disagree. I recently heard about a one-man exhibition at a prominent museum that featured a cropped photograph of an image in the exhibition announcement and related advertising. The artist had not been consulted and was upset. No legal or corrective action was taken, but the museum will be more careful in the future. The artist found the practice unethical.

Access: Direct and Indirect

Finding ways—physically, intellectually, or virtually—to optimize access to all the collections is an ethical obligation.[14]

What are the duties of a museum to allow people access to collections? In meeting these, what ethical concerns might there be? First, we must define access. Is it visual and at a distance, as might be the case for things which are on exhibit? Is it up close and physical, as might be the case for museum employees authorized to work with certain objects? In either circumstance accessibility will depend on the collection, the nature of access expectations, and the capabilities of the owning museum. There can be two kinds of collection access: direct and indirect.

Direct Access

Direct collection access usually means physical contact with or at least close proximity to items being studied, examined, or otherwise handled in some manner preapproved by the owning museum. Presumably this takes place under the supervision of responsible staff. Obviously, access can vary widely according to the objects being accessed. Automobiles require a different set of protections than butterflies.

Direct access usually requires considerable museum staff time to arrange and monitor. Only under certain circumstances can a nonemployee be left alone with collections. Ethically, a first concern in these scenarios is security. Collection loss must be guarded against. But collection damage must also be avoided. A person unqualified to handle a particular kind of collection could damage it. Some items require special conservation measures.

The ethics of direct access will depend on who is requesting it, why, for how long or often, and what resources the museum will need to devote to let it happen. Ethically, one might think anyone can have equal access to whatever collection the person is interested in. In practice that is rarely possible. Museums will have protective and intellectual criteria for those who get top access priority and for those relegated to a less privileged status. The ethics of who is allowed access to collections must be decided by a museum, not the person seeking access. Some people may think they are qualified to touch objects, yet museum staff may disagree.

Specific museum collections should be under the supervision of designated personnel trained to work with them. Materials requiring care would include textiles, photographs, automobiles, ceramics, paintings, furniture, archaeology findings, and the host of natural history specimens located in those institutions. Nonmuseum people seeking access can include members of the general public but only under the watchful care of assigned staff. Academic and research specialists may be allowed private access, but again, the outcome of such involvement must be monitored. Complaints can arise from people whose access is blocked for one reason or another. The complaint will be couched as an ethical violation: "Why can I not see such-and-such? I'm a citizen and my taxes support you (because museums are tax-exempt entities)."

Access in accord with the Americans with Disabilities Act is a major concern as all collections should be equally available to people, regardless of their physical ability. Without question, the most gratifying museum collection access I ever arranged happened at the Museum of the City of New York. One of the collections under my supervision was its small but impressive military material. This included medals of various sorts and dates. A researcher called to make an appointment to see the medals for a project. A time was set. When the person arrived, it turned out he was a severely disabled young man, in his late teens. He walked with great difficulty, and his hands were essentially nonfunctional. Clearly, he needed help handling the medal collection. I was happy to assist. He was from California and it was the first time his parents let him travel alone. He asked if he could photograph some of the medals. I waived our usual fees and agreed. He had a Minox camera. At the time, these were one of the smallest high-quality cameras on the commercial market. He had never used it, but it was easy to load the film and set up on a little tripod, which I did. When the photo shot was arranged, he tapped the shutter release. I have never seen a person emit such joy. What for most of us is a fairly mundane and ordinary act was for him a momentous accomplishment. The afternoon was heartwarming to say the least and simply confirmed the public service aspect of my definition of a museum.

Indirect Access

In January 2019, the Cleveland Museum of Art (CMA) announced a welcome form of indirect access to its collections. Its open access movement allows anyone to go on its website and navigate to see "as many as 30,000 CMA artworks that are in the public domain for commercial as well as scholarly and noncommercial purposes. Additional information on more than 61,000 artworks—both those in the public domain and those with copyright or other restrictions—is also now available" (appendix V).

It is obvious that more than a few ways of posting and supplying pictures became possible with the invention of computers and the internet. Museums were slow to jump on this visual bandwagon. Many have still not taken full advantage of ideal options when it comes to getting collections online. This measured pace is the result of meager financial resources, concerns about image piracy, fears of lost income, low prioritization, or misuse of collection reproductions.

Before the present internet opportunities existed, indirect collection access largely happened through hard copy image reproductions.

Collection and exhibition catalogues, books, slides, magazines, and other printed materials were essential tools for visual research. Happily, new technology has been of immense informational assistance for scholars and the general public alike. Yet, remember, knowledge still supersedes technology. The most sophisticated computers only hold scholarship, they cannot replace it.

Whether direct or indirect, the advent of easier access to collections has brought heightened ethics concerns. How will photos made by a museum visitor (my figure 4.1 image, for example) be used? What applications could unfold for pictures copied from a museum's website? Can, should, and how would a museum control the applications? What if my picture was photoshopped and everyone in the scene was given KKK headgear? Museum warnings about image uses may be posted in galleries and online, but these are more legal prophylactic measures for the museum itself rather than effective control measures. If anyone sees an offensive collection image, the pilloried museum can say it warned against such action.

Do museums have the ethical right to charge for access to, or any commercial visual use of, things in their collection? Museums hold their collections for the public good. In the United States, because museums are tax-exempt or tax-supported in some fashion, there can be an assumption that there should be no charge for collection access.

In Summary

Once a museum acquires something, it has an ethical obligation to assure collection stewardship and access. These duties are ongoing. As discussed, they are infused with ethics ramifications; from accurate and timely documentation to assuring proper storage to pursuing and allowing research, museum processes will vary according to an institution's mission, budget, personnel interests, governance priorities, and capabilities.

Collection stewardship and access is a wonderful concept, and one that most museums strive to achieve at various operational levels. Yet keeping and using things must not endanger collections. Museums are, first and foremost, conservation endeavors. What they acquire for public benefit has to be maintained and cared for in responsible ways. This preservation duty is generally referred to as conservation. An activity that was once a craft or maintenance activity, conservation is now an

ETHICS IN ACTION

1. I encountered a situation where a scholar demanded that a museum give her privileged and exclusive access to a particular manuscript collection until her research was completed and published. To the frustration of the scholar, I denied the arrangement. What would be the ethics concerns for such an arrangement and response?
2. The mayor of the town your museum is in has requested art for his office from the museum's permanent, accessioned collection. How should the museum respond to this, and what ethical issues might arise?
3. A reporter from the *New York Times* is investigating how museums receiving municipal appropriations care for their collections. She has requested access to the collection records and storage facilities of the museum you direct on Staten Island. How do you respond?
4. The board of trustees of the museum where you are the registrar has volunteered the museum to be a designated repository for archaeologically excavated material found in the town during surveys mandated when construction happens on government property. What ethical realities need to be understood and addressed in such an arrangement?

independent profession. It is a science and practice that, funding dependent, museums strive to embrace in spirit and apply in fact on the job. The ethics of conservation can be highly complex and individualistic. This is discussed in the following chapter.

Notes

1. Steven Lubar, *Inside the Lost Museum: Curating, Past and Present* (Cambridge, MA: Harvard University Press, 2017), 128.
2. Rebecca Buck and Jean Allman Gilman, *Museum Registration Methods,* 5th ed. (Washington, DC: The AAM Press, 2010).
3. Sally Yerkovich, *A Practical Guide to Museum Ethics* (Lanham, MD: Rowman & Littlefield, 2016), 49.
4. Gary Edson, *Museum Ethics in Practice* (New York: Routledge, 2017), 195.
5. Buck and Gilman, *Museum Registration Methods.*

6. Steven Miller, "Museum Storage: Out of Sight, Out of Mind," *Museum News,* January/February 2006, 57–59.

7. Christopher Kemp, *The Lost Species: Great Expeditions in the Collections of Natural History Museums* (Chicago: University of Chicago Press, 2017), xvii.

8. Ibid., xix.

9. Ibid., xx.

10. Douglas J. Preston, *Dinosaurs in the Attic: An Excursion into the American Museum of Natural History* (New York: St. Martin's Press, 1986), xi.

11. Nancy Rosoff, "Integrating Native Views into Museum Procedures: Hope and Practice at the National Museum of the American Indian," *Museum Anthropology* 22 (1998): 1–33, http://www.researchgate.net/publication/249427017_Integrating _Native_Views_into_museum_Procedures_Hope_and_Practice_at_the_National _Museum_of_the_American_Indian/citation/download.

12. Cornelia Dean, "A Rising Threat to History," *New York Times*, July 9, 2019, D1, D6.

13. MoMA Design Store, "Starry Night Umbrella Collapsible," https://store .moma.org/accessories/travel/starry-night-umbrella-collapsible/103540-103540 .html.

14. Tristram Besterman, "Museum Ethics," chapter 26 in *A Companion to Museum Studies,* ed. Sharon Macdonald (United Kingdom: Wiley-Blackwell, 2011), 437.

ETHICS AND
CONSERVATION

*Conservation is the profession devoted to preserving cultural material
for the future. By melding art with science, conservation protects our
heritage, preserves our legacy, and ultimately, saves our past for generations to come.*[1]

This chapter addresses the ethics of museum collection
conservation in application. The topic is presented and
amplified in a priority approach starting with defining the
responsibility of museums to care for the materials held by them in public trust. Commentary on conservation in application is outlined, especially for collection housing and handling. Issues are explained along
with corrective measures museums can encounter.

Defining Museum Collection Conservation

Museum collection conservation requires an unusual blend of knowledge
in science (especially chemistry), art history, and history, combined with
manual proficiencies. Defining museum conservation is the first priority
for any collecting institution. Museums must understand this discipline
as it relates to the sorts of materials they own and care for. In the United

States, the best way for nonconservators to learn about this is through the American Institute for Conservation of Historic and Artistic Works (AIC). This membership organization provides essential information, directives, and suggestions on contacts and behaviors essential to establishing and maintaining professional conservation approaches and practices.

In practice, museum collection conservation is a refined pursuit that takes years to learn. The ability to safely handle an often-puzzling assortment of materials, tools, and technologies is essential. This is not a field for distracted technophobes or blunderers. Patience is a virtue.

> Conservation today is a scientifically informed discipline guided by general principles as well as by a growing body of written information. This is not to suggest that conservation is a science. Scientific investigation and research have greatly contributed to a better understanding of the processes of deterioration and have provided safer methods of testing and treatment; however, only the sensitivity, knowledge, integrity, and skill of an individual can make possible a synthesis of science and art within the framework of ethical strictures that bound the practice to conservation.[2]

Most museums cannot afford their own conservation departments. Even large museums with conservation personnel may not have staff qualified to work with the full range of materials a museum owns. In either circumstance, outside conservators can usually help on a contract basis. Obviously, care must be exercised to assure competent professionals are hired. An essential subject when pursuing outside contractors will relate to the ethics of the museum and the potential conservator. Do these correspond? When speaking with references for a potential hire, always ask about a person's ethics and how they were reflected in his or her past work.

The AIC

With the development in the twentieth century of museum conservation as a unique profession came the creation in the United States of the AIC.[3] Other nations have similar bodies. It is a membership organization for the field and the go-to organization for information that museums may seek when dealing with conservation. It does not teach conservation but is a subject matter conduit.

Given the lengthy and sometimes tumultuous discussions that can surround conservation work, the AIC offers an excellent code of ethics for conservation and conservators (appendix VI). Few in the museum field truly understand the often complex philosophical and practical depth and scope of conservation. Even fewer people outside museums are aware of it. This is especially true for museum trustees. Formal discussions with conservators and museum representatives always prove beneficial prior to collection preservation projects.

Museum Conservation in Application

Museum conservation deals with ethics issues every day. As noted, a museum must define conservation for its particular purposes. A car museum might have different priorities than a stamp museum. It would be questionable to have an auto mechanic making decisions about how to house stamps for their best protection. Conversely, a stamp curator might not be the person to determine how to care for tires. Whatever a museum decides, collection conservation priorities need to be set along the following lines:

1. Examination: Before anything is done to an object its physical condition must be thoroughly assessed by a qualified conservator. This person may bring in specialists to assist with any analysis.
2. Documentation: All knowledge about an item must be recorded in an easily accessed hard copy and computerized manner, and for the long term.
3. Treatment: When qualified persons agree on what conservation measures should be done to and for an object, that process needs to be implemented as specified while recognizing that deviations may be required in response to unknown factors.
4. Preventive care: Once an object has been conserved it needs to be kept safely and accessibly for the long term.

Some conservation measures may be considered more ethical for an object than others. Naturally, one of the (*the?*) most important decisions to make is—who can properly address all the process requirements? Are they professionally qualified to do so? And, what are the ethics precepts they care about, know about, will follow, and will insist others follow?

Museum conservation seeks to meet two principles. What is done to an object must do no harm to it and every treatment should be able to be undone (i.e., reversed). In practice, both ideas may be unrealistic all the time. Nevertheless, they offer lofty ethical goals worth striving for.

Museum collection conservation focuses on two essential concerns:

- How collections are housed.
- How collections are handled.

Collection Housing

By providing the best storage possible, we are taking the first and most important step toward preserving our cultural heritage.[4]

Museum storage focuses on creating a neutral environment that will cause no harm to art, artifacts, specimens, etc. This is conservation by indirect action. Environmental matters include air quality, temperature and humidity controls, and protections from natural elements such as water, seismic shock, and light damage. Furnishings include shelving, racks, boxes, envelopes, and a host of things within which collections are contained. Neither buildings nor smaller housing materials should pose dangers to objects within them. There is ample information about these safety measures for many collection materials. It is totally unethical to keep collections in poor or threatening situations. Similar concerns involve actual buildings in cases when they constitute a museum's collection.

Collection Handling

It is imperative that anyone in physical contact with museum collections be qualified to do so without endangering them. Such contact includes touching objects in and for storage, as well as working on them in a conservation lab. This is direct conservation action. Its proper fulfillment is an ethical must. It will involve a small group of individuals. They tend to be curators, collection managers, designated maintenance and exhibition employees, and, of course, conservators. Because museum collections represent an incredible array of materials, often in an incredible mix of compositions, few individuals are equally trained to touch photographs, fossils, textiles, metals, painted surfaces, ceramics, rocks, glass, wood of any kind, stone, technological devices, taxidermy mounts, rubber, or cement, with authority. The conservation field tends to be divided into specialists with expertise in various material sciences and applications. It would be considered unethical to ask a painting conservator to work on a collection of mounted insects.

A cautionary note is always in order regarding who is qualified to do conservation work. Beware of people who claim experience but approach it as a craft activity. Some are amateurs at best or charlatans at worst. (Picture framing stores are especially weak painting conservation practitioners.) The AIC website offers excellent advice on seeking competent conservators. It is extraordinarily unethical for a museum to use an unqualified person to conduct any sort of conservation work.

Conservation Variables

Conservation discussions can and do go on at length. James Janowski in "The Moral Case for Restoring Artworks" offers an introduction to two approaches to conservation outcome decisions.[5] Janowski explains "purist restoration" and its opposite "integral restoration." One posits that restoration should never inject nonoriginal materials to a work of art even if the artwork appears poorly as a result of this inaction. The other places an emphasis on the appearance of an artwork and believes using nonoriginal materials is acceptable if they allow an artwork to at least appear original. Defining original and nonoriginal is an essential part of any discussion. Whatever the outcome, what decision is more ethical or less ethical? The answer is subjective and varies according to personal preference, prevailing cultural habits, and what the conservation field is thinking about at a particular time. In practice, it may seem there are few conservation ethics absolutes.

One argument offered by conservators is to leave objects alone and simply let them remain in storage or on exhibit without any conservation treatment. Jonathan Ashley-Smith offers insights into this approach in his essay "The Ethics of Doing Nothing." The piece explains how ethical arguments are applied to decide or decline conservation treatments.[6] Complaints about the adverse results of well-intentioned conservation treatment always lurk in the back of conservators' minds. It is one reason for the theory of reversibility. This approach to treating objects strives to make actions reversible insofar as materials and processes allow. For example, certain varnishes or other applications can be removed at a later date and presumably with no damage to the surface they once covered. The ethical ideal of reversibility is laudable if not always achievable.

A *New York Times* article about a 1955 painting by Willem de Kooning, *Woman-Ochre*, which was stolen from the University of Arizona Museum of Art in 1985, notes the discussions that unfolded during conservation treatment. The thieves cut it from the frame, rolled it up, and escaped undetected. The painting was recovered in 2017. In talking about how to bring the painting "back to near-original condition," a conservator discussing the project notes, "Once the painting is consolidated, cleaned and re-stretched, there will be endless debates with my team [and the Arizona museum staff] about retouching." "My instinct is that we are going to err toward maintaining the existing condition because that's where conservation is at the moment." In other words, there will be no attempt to make the picture look new.[7]

Conservation Issues

Whether it is an object in their own collections or something being considered for acquisition, museums must be alert for evidence of damaging, inauthentic, specious, or other alterations. This can be done by people who either are unqualified to take any physical action on an object or hope to "improve" its appearance and even make it worth more on the commercial market. How ethical such alterations are will depend on perspectives. If it is assumed that the work was done intentionally to deceive, that is clearly unacceptable. If, on the other hand, it was done innocently, less anger is expressed. There are many collecting areas that call for watchfulness. Furniture can be refinished, poorly repaired, or have its content changed to upgrade its historic value. Paintings can be badly in-painted, incorrectly relined, and even have signatures changed or added. Machinery is often subject to changes to make it operate or appear to be better than it was originally.

Over the years, paintings have often been the most physically abused of museum collections. The assaults happen both before and after a museum acquires them. Fortunately, with the rise of conservation as a distinct field of practice, museums cause less damage now. Paintings by the Cubists provide an easy example of mistakes that change how they were originally meant to be seen. "For it cannot be too strongly and too often emphasized that both Picasso and Braque were adamant that the surface of Cubist paintings be left matte and *never* in any circumstances varnished."[8]

In 2019, the *New York Times* exposed a huge controversy surrounding the baseball card collectors' market. In order to improve the commercial value of old trading cards, owners were sometimes cleaning them and cutting their rough edges so they appeared new. "Cards in pristine condition are highly valued by collectors and can fetch thousands of dollars more than similar cards with scuffs or worn edges. Sellers can improve the appearance of a card by trimming its edges or removing residue."[9] To date, these efforts appear to be the work of private owners and dealers alone. Qualified paper conservators, be they self-employed, on museum staff, or working with reputable independent conservation labs, have not been implicated in the practice.

The conservation of mechanical devices, small or large, is experiencing shifts in attitudes about approaches and outcomes. These adjustments largely reflect past collector preferences about how the things they own should look, and more importantly, operate. It was long thought that cars, clocks, machinery, and other technological materials should operate and appear as new as possible. Evidence of time, including rust, wear, previous owner upgrades, and other changes, was to be eradicated. Car collectors were, and many remain, the worst offenders. Indeed, their antique vehicles often look better than when they first rolled out of a factory. Mainstream scientific conservation approaches followed in the fine arts in particular have been slowly finding their way into the minds and actions of car collectors. The word "vintage" is now accepted as a collector category. The more original the materials and construction of a vehicle are, the more historically truthful it is. This is a titanic ethical shift in car collector thinking.

Conservation Corrections

Anyone who has visited conservation labs is aware of how decisions are made. The discipline occupies a rare intersection of concerns. Ethics are inevitably present in the mix. We need only look at the furor some people raised at the end of the last century about the conservation (primarily a cleaning process) of Michelangelo's Sistine Chapel frescoes. "The cleaning of art works raises the temperature of artistic debate more than any other subject."[10]

The Sistine ceiling frescoes are among the most famous works of art in the world. A major conservation project commenced in 1980, the results of which were unveiled by Pope John Paul II in 1994. They appeared visually dramatic and were not without complaints in that regard. The harshest critics were intransigent art historians who railed against the seemingly bright colors that emerged after hundreds of years of soot and grime had been carefully removed. It mattered little to the offended that when the art was new, descriptions of how strong the colors were had been clearly declared.[11]

In 2014, the decorative beard on the ancient gold burial mask of King Tutankhamen on exhibit in the Egyptian Museum, Cairo, Egypt, broke off when the object was being dusted by museum maintenance staff. The mask is of immense global renown. It was quickly glued back on—but not by staff qualified to do so. Customary museum conservation protocols were not followed. The glue used was an epoxy that was almost irreversible, meaning it was difficult to remove by museum conservators who were called in to correct the erroneous repair.[12]

Once people are accustomed to the particular look of art, change can be shocking. This is particularly true when an object is conserved in a manner that alters how it traditionally appeared. Complicating outcome opinions, conservation philosophies can be different for different things. Approaches regarding how to preserve automobiles, railroad engines, boats, airplanes, and large industrial artifacts are not necessarily the same as those for paintings, art on paper, ethnographic materials, or waterlogged wood artifacts.

Expert Commentary

It is arguably the first duty of museums to care for and preserve the collections, since these are the physical assets, owned by the public, for which the organization is accountable.[13]

Accusations of ethical affronts purposely committed by qualified, experienced, and knowledgeable museum conservators or their private sector colleagues are difficult to make with certainty. There can be uncertainty when trying to differentiate between conservation ethics or conservation mistakes. The two may or may not be linked. In speaking about mistakes made in conservation, Isabelle Brajer, painting conservator at the National Museum of Denmark, notes that "the understanding of what a mistake is can be viewed differently depending on one's perspectives. Mistakes can cover such concepts as oversights, misconceptions, and misinterpretations, and can affect both the theoretical and practical decision-making processes."[14] She knows conservators work not only with objects and materials but with ideas and information. Uncertainty, innocent ignorance, and authoritarian directives that force conservators to do work in a way they would not are declining influences on conservation results. Fortunately, ethical transgressions are therefore also on the decline.

The following comment by Jonathan Kemp, a sculpture conservator in England, neatly summarizes conservation ethics from within the profession: "As it is, codes of ethics are intended to produce agreed behaviors. Within conservation they do so not by invoking clearly defined goals, rather by providing aspiration guidelines in treatment decision-making and reflect, albeit perhaps by consensus, the guiding philosophy of the conservation constituency."[15] The best introduction to conservation for the layperson is the book *Historical and Philosophical Issues in the Conservation of Cultural Heritage*.[16] This is not a hands-on instruction manual but an in-depth compilation of essays by art historians, museum curators, and directors, as well as conservation scientists and practitioners. It presents philosophical views on conservation ethics that can be quite complex and variable.

In Summary

Once the often-complicated nature of conservation is understood and accepted by a museum, applying its realities unfolds on many levels. As discussed, conservation unfolds on two fronts: (1) in actions taken to objects; and (2) in assuring a safe environment for them, before, during, or after any action happens. Points presented explain how the field has advanced from that of a craft to that of a highly specialized academic as well as manual discipline. Considerable experience and knowledge are required to safely and correctly address conservation issues, but even currently acceptable approaches will, in time, be found wanting. This is, naturally, why the objectives of being able to reverse applications and assure that no damage is done to museum collections by a particular process are so important. Conservation concerns are especially sensitive when doing exhibitions. The following chapter discusses the broader ethical perspectives of this most public part of museum work. Conservation is just one of many things to address when deciding exhibit topics, object selection and presentation, and how to deal with any complaints that

ETHICS IN ACTION

1. You are the collection manager of a regional museum of art. It has no conservator on staff but relies on contractors to advise or address collection conservation matters. The contractors must be members in good standing of the American Institute for Conservation. A large eighteenth-century portrait from the permanent collection has been given to a highly-qualified painting conservator for treatment. The sitter was a famous person from your community. The artist is unknown. It is oil on canvas. The painting was damaged years ago and "fixed" by a local artist when he was a student in art school. His father was on the museum's board of trustees at the time. The artist is now on that board. The painting conservator has examined the piece and submitted a treatment proposal. Among its recommendations is correcting what it characterizes as previous highly flawed restoration work. How will the museum decide what to have done and what sort of ethics matters need to be considered in making the decision?

2. A museum is accepting a ceramic plaque landscape picture in its original frame, dating to circa 1917. It measures 8 x 10 and was made by the Rookville Pottery Co. While there is an overall mild craquelure pattern, the piece is in otherwise acceptable original condition, though dirty. An antiques dealer has advised the owner on how to clean the plaque before making the donation. Does this raise any ethical concerns for the museum, and if so what might they be and what action, if any, should the museum take and how?

3. Given the vast range of materials that museum objects are made of, how can an institution set a feasible conservation policy?

emerge. When public debates erupt regarding museum exhibitions, they can be quite vitriolic. They are always based on accusations of unethical behavior by a museum.

Notes

1. American Institute for Conservation, "What Is Conservation," http://www.culturalheritage.org.

2. Konstanze Bachmann, introduction to *Conservation Concerns: A Guide for Collectors and Curators* (New York: Cooper-Hewitt National Museum of Design, Smithsonian Institution, 1992), 2.

3. American Institute for Conservation of Historic and Artistic Works, www.culturalheritage.org.

4. Konstanze Bachmann and Rebecca Anne Rushfield, "Principles of Storage," in *Conservation Concerns: A Guide for Collectors and Curators,* ed. Konstanze Bachmann (New York: Cooper-Hewitt National Museum of Design, Smithsonian Institution, 1992), 5.

5. James Janowski, "The Moral Case for Restoring Artworks," chapter 10 in *Ethics and the Visual Arts,* ed. Elaine A. King and Gail Levin (New York: Allworth Press, 2006), 143–54.

6. Jonathan Ashley-Smith, "The Ethics of Doing Nothing," *Journal of the Institute of Conservation*, 41, no. 1 (2018): 6–15, https://www.tandfonline.com/doi/full/10.1080/19455224.2017.1416650.

7. Jori Finkel, "Coming-Out Party for Kidnapped de Kooning," *New York Times*, March 14, 2019, C5.

8. John Richardson, "Crimes Against the Cubists," *Historical and Philosophical Issues in the Conservation of Cultural Heritage* (Los Angeles: J. Paul Getty Trust, 1996), 186.

9. Paul Sullivan, "Retouching the Mona Lisa Is Restoration, but a Mickey Mantle? Collectors Cry Fraud," *New York Times*, June 14, 2019, https://www.nytimes.com/2019/06/14/your-money/sports-cards-alteration-fraud.html.

10. Paul Taylor, *Condition: The Ageing of Art* (London: Paul Holberton, 2015), 195.

11. M. Kirby Talley Jr., "Michelangelo Rediscovered: The Sistine Chapel Born Again," *ARTNews*, Summer, 1987, 159–70.

12. Faith Karini, "Eight People Face Charges Over Broken King Tut Mask," CNN.com, updated January 28, 2016, https://www.cnn.com/2016/01/24/africa/king-tut-broken-mask-charges/index.html.

13. Suzanne Keene, *Managing Conservation in Museums,* 2nd ed. (Oxford, England and Woburn, MA: Butterworth-Heinemann, 2002), 139.

14. Isabelle Brajer, "Taking the Wrong Path: Learning from Oversights, Misconceptions, Failures and Mistakes in Conservation," *CeROArt. Conservation,*

Exposition, Restauration d'Objets d'Art, Revue electronique, 3 (2009), https:// journals.openedition.org/ceroart/1127#octo1n1.

15. Jonathan Kemp, "Practical Ethics v2.0," in *Conservation Principles, Dilemmas and Uncomfortable Truths*, ed. Alison Richmond and Alison Bracker (London and New York: Routledge, 2011), 60–72.

16. Nicholas Stanley Price, M. Kirby Talley, and Alessandra Melucco Vaccaro, eds. *Historical and Philosophical Issues in the Conservation of Cultural Heritage* (Los Angeles: Getty Publications, 1996).

EXHIBITION ETHICS

We are accustomed to think of the century just ended as one of great success in public communications. It was the century of radio, television, cinema, the recording industry, the fax machine and finally the internet. Yet there is still another success story in public communications that remains with us and is constantly growing and extending its influence—the museum.[1]

Exhibitions are the most public aspect of museum work. Implementing them can range from easy to complex. Whether they are small or large, temporary or long term, out of the ordinary or traditional, ethical considerations can infuse just about all aspects of exhibition development. This chapter discusses exhibition ethics in application—from deciding on a topic, to object selection, to design, to installation, and, when the occasion arises, to controversy.

The Exhibition as Communication Medium

The public communication medium "unique to the museum" is the exhibition.[2] Exhibitions convey their messages through a stand-alone physical visual medium that mixes objects, light, sound, words, architecture (existing or new), as well as graphic and spatial design elements. Exhibits pick up where old grade school show-and-tell exercises left off.

Exhibits are not always easy to do. Even simple displays involve considerable thought about intellectual and physical content, location, appearance, and associated programming. To one degree or another, ethical concerns relate to all aspects of organization and presentation.

Topic

Considerations in play when deciding on exhibit themes are usually quite simple. What can a museum show in its galleries that will, to one degree or another, inform, delight, entertain, assure, or reassure? Ethics plays an implied or overt role. It is expected that museums will show art, artifacts, and specimens that are about their mission. This charge is seen in tens of thousands of exhibits. While most topics are appropriate and obvious, some can cause public dissent. For example, in certain contexts nudity might be offensive and thus considered unethical. In other contexts, it may seem natural.

Deciding on a museum exhibition topic can involve two major questions about why they exist: Are they places of entertainment, or are they places of education? Visitors may see "'enjoyment' coming to mind more frequently than 'education'"[3] Are these interests ethically opposed? No. Museums have been superb at blending the two. People can learn and have a pleasant experience at the same time. Finances and mission-driven intellectual rigor are the whips that help control any amusement park inclinations exhibit designers might have. Concerns about display folderol aside, two critical content aspects must be known if an exhibition is reasonably feasible: Is there adequate information on the topic, and what objects will convey this information?

Object Selection

Deciding what objects an exhibition will contain can happen before, during, or after an exhibition topic is decided upon. Ethics outcomes of any selection will depend on the nature of an exhibit and how suitable visual content will be for an audience or audiences. What circumstances are required to get and show particular items? For example: Will there be obvious conflicts of interest with lenders? Are there unrealistic loan fees? Will the museum be required to pay for conservation treatment? Are there exhibition format restrictions? Are there ownership issues? Are the items sought actually available? On the surface, these and other considerations might seem only of practical concern. Museums must be on guard from beginning to end when it comes to deciding what to exhibit. Objects that once might have been acceptable to show can become unacceptable, but in time they can revert back to being acceptable. Museum staff must be cognizant of evolving social, cultural, and political community sensitivities. This, of course, requires defining community.

A perfect example of vacillating museum collection exhibition ethics can be found at the Museum of the City of New York. It has one of the largest collections of lithographs by the nineteenth-century Manhattan sequential firms of N. Currier and Currier & Ives. The museum owns about three thousand of the approximately nine thousand images the companies produced. (These were multiples and not numbered limited editions.) When most people think of Currier productions, the bucolic winter snow scenes immediately come to mind as they have been reproduced for decades on Christmas cards, especially. Moreover, there is hardly an aspect of America's history for which a print by either company is not used for illustrative purposes in all sorts of publications. Until recently, though, there was one aspect of the art that was hardly ever seen.

Towards the end of Currier & Ives operations, when both principals were deceased, a series of race cartoons were made that depicted a mythical African American community called Darktown. Most people now see these as highly offensive depictions of blacks pursuing various activities. A caption for one explains the tone of all. The print shows two contestants in an oyster-eating contest along with a few judges and piles of oyster shells. The caption reads: "Great Oyster Eating Match Between the Darktown Cormorant and the Blackville Buster. The Finish—"Yous is a tie—De one dat gags fust, am a gone Coon."

When I was a young, aspiring curator at the museum and working with its picture collections, these prints were never exhibited. Times have changed for museums regarding collections they own that show derogatory racial, ethnic, and gender images. Current practice makes it more acceptable to present these when interpreted in the context of the times in which they were created. The Darktown prints are now included in books about Currier & Ives as well as in exhibits. This visual record is important evidence of an aspect of history that is no longer hidden. The ethics of how such collections are kept and used by museums are being reconsidered.

Exceptions aside, the vast majority of things selected for museum exhibitions never cause difficulties. Visitors believe whatever is placed on view is there for a relevant purpose. They understand and accept curatorial decisions regarding both object and information content. Though hardly a single factor in exhibition-making, given the neutral nature of most presentations, museums are rarely concerned about ruffling visitor feathers. Yet, as discussed further, controversy can happen.

Location

Ethics and deciding what space to use for a museum exhibition may seem unrelated but they are not. "A good exhibition does not ignore the idiosyncrasies of its site: it either exploits them to unexpected effect, or makes them disappear to the measure possible."[4] Museum architecture may attempt to accommodate every kind of exhibition. Over time, that one-size-fits-all approach rarely works. Complaints about display outcomes can be especially strong coming from living artists featured in a museum show.

I have worked with scores of contemporary artists. So far, my curating has not caused disputes. This is mostly the result of very clear and lengthy pre-exhibit explanations regarding a museum's exhibit design process, what spaces will be allocated for what specific work, who will install the pieces and how they are to be arranged, and who writes and edits word-based materials, etc. In a few cases, artists who were good at showing their work effectively were invited to participate (without holding the museum legally liable for anything).

Exhibit Design Ethics

Museums regularly update how collections are shown. A simple example from the past would be an abstract painting hung upside down, which is not only an optical faux pas but an ethical offense.[5] Exhibit designers are critical visual thinkers, and most are sensitive to optimum display manners. A current concern involves costume exhibits. Mannequins are a special focus for ethics reasons. For years they have been used frequently in various practical capacities at art, history, and archaeology and anthropology museums. Their appearance has changed dramatically in recent decades. What once looked like white or beige cheap department store display torsos on wobbly metal stands now come in highly crafted (and expensive) color and figural options. From deep flat black to bright, shiny white hues, the rainbow implications hold up well under all sorts of applications. Lengthy discussions ensue among exhibit designers, curators, directors, and preparators about how and if arms, legs, hands, and heads are to be included on mannequins. The result can cause ethics attacks, so care is cautioned.

"Due to their role in disseminating knowledge of racial differences, ethnographic mannequins—particularly the ones with distinct facial features—can be considered controversial and problematic."[6] In a revealing chapter on an Asian costume exhibit, Tom Kolbe notes, "Costume exhibitions present particular installation challenges because each garment requires individual attention and custom display techniques. Conventional mannequins, with their idealized proportions and Western features, proved inappropriate for an exhibition of Asian costumes."[7] We saw how the Philadelphia Museum of Art handled mannequin challenges in its 2018 exhibition *Fabulous Fashion: From Dior's New Look to Now* (figure 10.1).

Figure 10.1. *Fabulous Fashion: From Dior's New Look to Now,* Philadelphia Museum of Art, 2018. Photo by Steven Miller © 2018

Interpretation Ethics

Museums are in the explanation business. In the trade this is known as interpretation. It is largely done through exhibitions. Most are presented without being the target of ethics debate. This happens for three reasons: museums are good at showing exhibits well; most exhibitions are generally benign; if controversial subjects and objects are to be presented, organizers usually prepare for this in advance. Occasionally there are surprises.

For years when the Museum of the City of New York exhibited an eighteenth-century American portrait of a prominent member of a minority religious group, it neglected to explain in the label copy that he made his fortune in the slave trade. The label simply noted the usual succinct information listing his name and life dates, the artist and his dates, the medium, and the donor of the picture. Eventually this biographical lapse was corrected when the painting was exhibited with a longer and more informative label in a new display, for which the author was the curator.

Periodically an object is explained incorrectly in a museum exhibition. A recent example involves a ceramic elongated orb-shaped object dating back some 4,500 years. It was on view at the British Museum and presented as a bowl or vase from what is now southern Iraq. Research from 2019 discovered it is actually a ceremonial mace head of the same period and place of origin. It would have been attached to a handheld pole as a war club. Ignorance of collections is not necessarily unethical but a refusal to correct mistakes when they become known is. The museum announced its error and changed the display.

Historic House Exhibition Ethics

Historic house museums can present peculiar dichotomies when it comes to the ethics of interpretation. Often, these structures have been preserved by communities because they hold historical meaning about a place. Their age alone can cause them to be saved. They might have architectural importance. Or, they were owned or occupied by an important person(s). These buildings are usually divided into two kinds: those that have original furnishings and those that do not.

Preserved historic houses with original furnishings include the home of Franklin D. Roosevelt, National Historic Site, in Hyde Park, New York; Graceland, Elvis Presley's mansion in Memphis, Tennessee; and Olana, the Catskill, New York, home of the nineteenth-century Hudson River School painter, Frederic Church. These buildings and their contents are of a piece, each being as important as the other. The ethics of preserving these sites as a whole requires that they keep their original contents. As a result, few things are removed, replaced, or dramatically altered. They stand as evidence. The ethics mission of each home is confirmed by the authentic décor, not just the structure itself.

Important house museums with furnishings not original to them include most of the homes in Historic Deerfield, Deerfield, Massachusetts; the Tenement Museum in New York City; and Boscobel House and Gardens in Garrison, New York. These hold objects original to the historic eras of each place. Items were, and still are, assembled by curators seeking to create a sense of what it was like to live in a certain setting at a certain time. The results are quite accurate and believable. Is this generally accepted curatorial practice ethical? The answer, of course, is—it depends. If the interpretation of such places is honest, the pretend nature of the furnishings is explained in all publicity, tour, and other word-based materials generated by the museum. It is unethical to state or suggest otherwise.

Contemporary Art and Exhibit Ethics

There are three ways to compliment artists: buy their art, exhibit it, do both. Being a museum curator and director often gave me the opportunity to choose option three. It was always an optimum ethical choice. I am hardly alone as thousands of like-minded museum employees certainly share a similar enthusiasm for art makers. Indeed, for the famous British art historian and museum director Kenneth Clark (1903–1983), "there was one group who could do no wrong: the artists. His patience with them exceeded anything possible in the other compartments of his life."[8]

Working with living artists will involve ethics conversations. Whether the art is owned by or lent to a museum, discussions will hover around how pieces are selected and shown. A positive rapport with artists is always beneficial for a museum. Problems can work against relationships with an art community, especially on local levels. Usually, museums and artists get along well. Naturally, there are exceptions, and these can reek of ethics violations or accusations thereof.

Recently, a foundation gave a historic house museum in the northeastern United States an outdoor sculpture installation and a ten-year maintenance grant to sustain it. The sculpture consists of a series of cast bronze portrait busts on matching pedestals in a specific garden setting. The sculptor is an accomplished artist. He not only made the art and installed it but designed and created the site. He was given full authority to do this well in advance of his work. His plan was approved by the then director and its board of trustees. The entire project cost the museum nothing and the annuity was a budget asset.

Following the retirement of the director but well before the project was completed, the museum's new director abruptly decided to radically change the site's landscaping. This was summarily accomplished without any prior discussions with the artist or the foundation. There was no logical reason for the change. When the artist and foundation were alerted (not by the museum) and inquired, both were shocked about the alteration. The violation was brought to their attention when the landscape company they hired to tend the site arrived one day only to find the garden configuration completely leveled. It was, to say the least, insulting for the artist and his exhibit. The resulting alteration is a clear ethical breech.

Exhibition installation ethics questions occasionally surface when display techniques alter the visual integrity of an object. Figure 10.2 shows a folding screen on view in a temporary exhibit at an East Coast regional American art museum. To stabilize the screen and protect it from being accidentally jarred or even knocked over, a 6-foot-long, 1.5-inch-diameter wood dowel was nested into the corner of two screen panels and anchored through a hole in the exhibit base. Several questions come to mind: Did it interfere with visually reading the screen as conceived and made? Were alternative, less obvious security methods considered? Was it necessary at all? The safety measure may have been effective, but was it ethical?

Dioramas were once quite popular teaching tools for museums. At their most dramatic, they were meticulously crafted life-size re-creations of historic or natural history scenes and environs. They were designed to make viewers feel present in the wild or in a past time and place. Some included museum collections. Others held things made expressly for the scene. As with certain historic houses, over time, dioramas have taken

Figure 10.2. Folding screen by Mark Sfirri (b. 1952) and Robert Dodge (b. 1939), 1989. Temporary Exhibition, Michener Art Museum, Doylestown, PA, March 8, 2019. Photo by Steven Miller © 2019

on the status akin to accessioned museum collection objects. There has been debate about retaining this old-fashioned form of museum teaching. Consequently, there are fewer dioramas than once was the case.

The American Museum of Natural History is famous for its dioramas. One has been given updated interpretive information. There is a full-scale scene of American Indians meeting with Dutch settlers in lower Manhattan. The diorama was made in 1939. It reflects a white Eurocentric view of how the indigenous peoples would have looked and what gender roles they would have played. New labeling follows complaints about inaccuracies and omissions (e.g., no canoes on the water can be seen in the distance where Dutch ships are, though they surely would have been in evidence at the time). The updated information appears on the glass through which visitors view the scene. The change resulted from internal museum research and a few years of discussions with current representatives of historic tribes, such as the Lenape. It was a result "of protests by members of Decolonize This Place, a movement urging institutions to acknowledge the struggles of Indigenous peoples and other groups asking the museum to change demeaning displays."[9]

Sources of financial support for exhibitions can be lightning rods for ethics complaints. Though tangentially connected to collections, care is advised when seeking money from certain contributors. In the 1970s and 1980s, the Phillip Morris Company, whose major product was tobacco, was an underwriter of museum exhibitions. As the health risks of smoking finally began to be acknowledged, fewer museums sought money from the firm. In time, even the corporate executives realized how damaging their industry was and the company changed its name to Altria. A similar example of ethics complaints about museum funding sources is unfolding at the time of this writing. Purdue Pharma, makers of pain killers containing the highly addictive OxyContin, is owned by the Sackler family. The family has been a generous funder of various museum exhibits, buildings, and programs. Because of demonstrations against the family and its philanthropy, museums that previously received its support are declining or even returning the funds.[10]

Exhibition Ethics Controversy

There have been several prominent examples of art museum exhibits that attracted harsh criticism. In 1990, a traveling exhibition of photographs by Robert Mapplethorpe was held at the Contemporary Arts Center of Cincinnati. It was entitled *The Perfect Moment*. Several images were suggestively homoerotic and caused local authorities to claim the museum was showing pornography. Legal charges were brought against the director. The ensuing trial found in favor of the museum, absolving it of unethical practices.[11]

In 1999, the Brooklyn Museum hosted *Sensation*, a traveling exhibit of new art from a private collection. One picture attracted the ire of Rudolph Giuliani, who was mayor of New York City at the time. Roman Catholic Church leaders chimed in as did others who were offended. The painting was done by Chris Ofili, who entitled it *The Holy Virgin Mary*. The image depicted an African woman and included elephant dung as part of the materials. The mayor threatened to remove the city's annual financial support for the museum if it was not taken down. He had no unilateral authority to take the action and nothing happened.[12]

In March 2019, the Children's Museum of Indianapolis removed three items related to the pop star Michael Jackson. His alleged pedophilia caused the museum to decline keeping them on view.[13]

Remains of deceased humans are now treated quite differently in museum exhibitions than they were in the past. Showing human skeletal or other specimens calls for special care. *Bodies . . . The Exhibition*, organized by a commercial exhibition company and shown at various venues across the United States, featured original figures of dead people in various postures. The skin had been removed to show bodily systems. It was quite popular, but it also elicited considerable controversy. The bodies were from China and questions arose over the propriety of presenting them without confirmed provenance regarding individual or familial permission to do so.[14] Museums declined the exhibition for ethical reasons.

In an essay published by the Institute for Cultural Practices at the University of Manchester in England, Caitlin LaPorte wrote in 2014: "The issue of displaying human remains in museums is one that I find very interesting because there is no right or wrong way of going about it."[15]

Shrunken heads are commonly found in older ethnology museums including the Smithsonian Institution's Natural History Museum (Washington, DC), Quai Branly (Paris), and the Ethnographic Museum (Berlin). Most were collected by foreigners in Peru and Ecuador from the 1870s into the 1930s. Considerable international discussions are

ETHICS IN ACTION

1. In 2019, the Museum of the American Revolution in Philadelphia, Pennsylvania, presented an exhibition of forty original antique thirteen-star American flags. As explained on the museum's website: "The exhibit was developed and curated by Jeff R. Bridgeman, a leading dealer of antique flags and political textiles, from his collection of historic flags." What, if any, ethical issues might the exhibit cause?

2. You are a museum's art collection curator. One of the collections for which you are responsible includes a large group of watercolor paintings by an artist who is popular in your region. The museum is known for these pictures. The artist is gay, and some of his work depicts sex between males. What ethics concerns will the museum have regarding how these are shown, in either exhibition or other ways?

3. The southern town where your museum is located is removing a statue honoring Confederate soldier residents from that town who died in the American Civil War. The town government, which owns your museum, has decided to move the statue to your grounds and require it be on display there. What ethics considerations, if any, need be addressed when it is reerected?

4. A recent example of the ethics of how the Holocaust is treated was discussed when planning an exhibition, *Persecution of the Jews in Photographs: The Netherlands 1940–1945*, presented in 2019 at the National Holocaust Museum, Amsterdam, and at the Topographie des Terrors in Berlin in 2019–2020. Speaking of the decision to show highly disturbing pictures, Emile Schrijver, "the general director of the organization that runs the National Holocaust Museum and other Jewish cultural sites in Amsterdam," noted, "If we are going to show images like these, the context has to be 100 percent historically correct." "We're not afraid to show them, but we feel we show them in the context that we believe is necessary, which also contains a discussion on how to deal with them."[1] What do you think he means by "context" insofar as exhibition ethics are concerned?

NOTE

1. Nina Siegal, "Witnessing Wartime Persecution Through Dutch Eyes," *New York Times*, May 31, 2019, C2.

underway about the ethics of having and exhibiting them, not to mention how they were acquired by collectors. In England, "the Pitt Rivers Museum is reconsidering its display of shrunken heads."[16]

An example from 2018 of new approaches to human skeleton displays in museums took place at the Mütter Museum of the College of Physicians of Philadelphia. Carol Orzel suffered from fibrodysplasia ossificans progressive. Upon death she wanted her skeleton to be donated to the museum. The museum agreed, and it is now on exhibit along with her identity and disease information. Clearly, this was considered an ethical arrangement by both the deceased donor and the museum. The museum's collections emphasize anatomical specimens and associated historical medical instruments. There is an extensive related library. The museum dates to 1863.[17]

In Summary

Museums have long been careful about exhibition ethics. For social, political, financial, and cultural reasons, those responsible for organizing exhibitions veer from subjects or content that might cause complaints. When controversy happens, museums need to be secure in the mission logic of the exhibit that was attacked, and honestly and quickly respond. The problem should be seen as an opportunity to educate both the museum and the attackers, not to mention uninvolved observers. An excellent book on the topic is Steven C. Dubin's *Displays of Power: Controversy in the American Museum from the Enola Gay to Sensation.*[18]

The problems of exhibition ethics debates involve the voluntary or involuntary loss of museum collections. In the past, it was assumed that what museums owned, especially as seen in their exhibits, would be held by them in perpetuity. Increasingly, we know this is not always the case. The next chapter delves into what can be a dicey ethics conundrum.

Notes

1. Barry Lord, "The Purpose of Museum Exhibitions," in *The Manual of Museum Exhibitions,* ed. Barry Lord and Gail Dexter Lord (Lanham, MD: AltaMira Press, Rowman & Littlefield, 2002), 11.
2. Ibid., 12.
3. Ibid., 15.

4. Robert Storr, "Show and Tell," in *What Makes A Great Exhibition?*, ed. Paula Marincola (Philadelphia, PA: Philadelphia Exhibitions Initiative, The Pew Center for Arts & Heritage, 2006), 29.

5. Sarah Cascone, "This Day in History: The Museum of Modern Art Hung a Matisse Upside Down and No One Noticed," *artnetNews*, October 18, 2016, https://news.artnet.com/exhibitions/moma-hangs-matisse-upside-down-683900.

6. Brita Brenna, Hans Dam Christensen, and Olav Hamran, *Museums as Cultures of Copies: The Crafting of Artefacts and Authenticity* (New York: Routledge, Taylor & Francis & Group, 2018), 28.

7. Tom Klobe, "The Art of Asian Costume," *Exhibitions: Concept, Planning and Design* (Washington, DC: The AAM Press of American Association of Museums, 2012), 146.

8. James Stourton, *Kenneth Clark: Life, Art and Civilisation* (New York: Knopf, 2016), 111.

9. Ana Fota, "Revisions Give a Diorama a New Story," *New York Times*, March 20, 2019, C1, C6.

10. ABC Radio, "Sackler Family Pausing Donations as Top Museums Cut Ties to OxyContin Maker," WTOP, March 26, 2019, https://wtop.com/dc/2019/03/sackler-family-pausing-donations-as-top-museums-cut-ties-to-oxycontin-maker/.

11. Wikipedia, "The Perfect Moment," Wikipedia, last edited July 29, 2019, https://en.wikipedia.org/wiki/The_Perfect_Moment.

12. Wikipedia, "*The Holy Virgin Mary*," Wikipedia, last edited May 4, 2019, https://en.wikipedia.org/wiki/The_Holy_Virgin_Mary.

13. Caroline Goldstein, "As Allegations Against Michael Jackson Swirl, One Children's Museum Removes All Its Memorabilia of the Singer," Artnet.com, March 18, 2019, https://news.artnet.com/art-world/michael-jackson-memorabilia-removed-childrens-museum-1490800.

14. Chris Bergeron, "Bodies Exhibit Popular, but Is It Ethical?" *MetroWest Daily News*, October 23, 2007, https://www.metrowestdailynews.com/x357660633.

15. Caz103, "Ethics of Displaying Human Remains in Museums by Caitlin LaPorte," Institute for Cultural Practices, University of Manchester, November 26, 2019, https://culturalpractice.wordpress.com/2014/11/26/ethics-of-displaying-human-remains-in-museums-by-caitlin-laporte/.

16. Martin Bailey, "Oxford Museum Rethinks Famed Display of Shrunken Heads," *The Art Newspaper*, March 6, 2019, https://www.theartnewspaper.com/news/oxford-museum-rethinks-famed-display-of-shrunken-heads. An excellent history of how the heads of dead humans have been used, including by museums, is discussed in Frances Larson, *Severed: A History of Heads Lost and Heads Found* (New York: W. W. Norton, 2014).

17. Marie McCullough, "Her Skeleton Stands as a Testimony to Her Resilience," *The Philadelphia Inquirer*, March 1, 2019, A1, A6.

18. Steven C. Dubin, *Displays of Power: Controversy in the American Museum from the Enola Gay to Sensation* (New York: NYU Press, 1999).

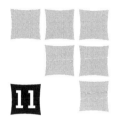

ETHICS AND COLLECTION LOSS

There is much we don't know about what happened this month [April 2003] at the Baghdad Museum, at its National Library and archives, at the Mosul museum and the rest of that country's gutted cultural institutions.[1]

Expanding rather than shrinking collections is the norm for most museums. Yet, there are times when collection losses happen. This takes place by museums themselves or can be caused by forces beyond their control. Either form of loss is intertwined with ethics concerns. This chapter explains the most common forms of these occurrences and their ethics ramifications. It is divided into two parts. The first explains why and how museums deliberately choose to remove things from their collections. The second half discusses collection losses over which museums have no influence.

Deliberate Museum Collection Loss

Occasionally, museums voluntarily remove collections from ownership. The action is called deaccessioning. On the surface, this may seem to contradict why museums exist. Acquiring and keeping valued objects is a core practice, not getting rid of them. However, collection subtraction has taken place since museums were invented. In the past, this was largely unremarked upon. Recently, the practice has received considerable attention. Today, museums include deaccessioning policies and activities on websites, in annual reports, and with notifications of sales, exchanges, donations to other institutions, or combinations thereof.

Most museums have deaccession instructions in their collection management policies. Local and national museum profession membership organizations have codes to abide by. These are listed on their websites. Three prominent groups are the American Alliance of Museums (www.aam-us.org), the American Association for State and Local History (www.aashl.org), and the Association of Art Museum Directors (www.aamd.org).[2] Because the majority of museums are private and own their collections without restrictions, they usually have the legal right to do with them as they wish. However, the ethics of why and how they delete collections can be debated outside these institutions.

Why a museum removes something can cause serious ethics questions. Controversy often erupts over one of two questions, or both: Why is a museum getting rid of an object? If it is being sold, how will the income be used? Reasons for museum collection reductions range from acceptable to specious, as noted in the textbox on the following page.

When it comes to removing collections, decisions should be made with thoughtful deliberation and in a carefully prescribed way. The ethics of any and all actions need to be examined. Customarily, deaccessioning is carried out with the approval and direction of boards of trustees. The process should start with knowledgeable staff recommendations. These, in turn, are generally based on acceptable explanations listed above. Poor deaccession arguments reflect unethical behavior.

Voices inside a museum or the field generally can caution against the practice, or at least how it is applied, but those opinions are rarely expressed publicly. Employees wish to stay employed. Final decisions are always made, or at least approved, by boards of trustees over whom staff have no authority. Moreover, trustees increasingly initiate the removals. They tend to do so for anything but scholarly reasons.

To address apparent and understandable ethics contradictions in the public's mind, museums need to do everything within their power to provide honest and transparent explanations of their actions. These will be especially important should there be a vociferous condemnation

DEACCESSIONING ARGUMENTS

- Generally Acceptable Deaccessioning Arguments
  An item is:
  - Outside a museum's mission
  - Poses an untenable retention cost
  - Subject to ownership dispute
  - Illegal to own
  - A collection duplicate
  - Redundant (there are more than enough examples in a particular category)
  - A fake or forgery
  - A copy or reproduction
  - Of poor physical quality, self-destructing
  - A safety threat
  - Appropriate for another museum
  - A violation of a conflict-of-interest policy
  - A combination of above reasons
- Specious Deaccessioning Arguments
  An item:
  - Is unpopular with an employee or trustee
  - Is an intellectual orphan—there is a lack of information about it
  - Has not been exhibited
  - Is desired by a private individual
  - Is a source of potential income

of deaccessioning. When discussing deaccessioning, it is important to acknowledge at least one of four observations.

- Most museum collections are probably not being considered for removal.
- Deaccessioning has, since the mid-1970s, been accepted within the museum field as a viable, and ethical, collection management practice.
- When deaccessioning happens commercially, meaning an object is sold, the proceeds are to be allocated for new acquisitions or to pay for the direct care of existing collections. This is a recommendation within the museum field.

- Questions are beginning to arise that suggest unbridled deaccessioning by sale with no protections for the object in question contradicts a fundamental museum ethics tenant regarding the preservation of the things held in trust by these institutions for past, present, and it is hoped, future generations. The outcome of this conversation is inter-museum transfer by sale or donation. It is considered a highly ethical form of deaccessioning.

Customary Deaccession Process

In defining museum-initiated collection removals, it is important to understand customary internal processes for the action. There are optimum ways to purposely delete collections. The process should be clearly outlined in a museum's collection policies and referenced in other documents.

- Ideally, a deaccession suggestion starts with the curator or an individual with a knowledge base regarding the object or objects in question. These individuals must understand the context of the prospective departing item within the museum's history and mission and collection scope.
- Political and social sensitivities should be examined regarding donors of objects being slated for removal. Donors can be people who gave an item, or funds to purchase it. It is unwise to alienate these contributors. It is also unwise to jeopardize future collection gifts through capricious deaccessioning. Donors will not give to museums if the long-term survival of their donations is precarious.
- There will be occasions when a museum's governing authority, typically a board of trustees, will decide on significant individual or large-scale deaccessions.
- Expressing objections to a deaccessioning should be permitted within an institution while the action is being considered. A museum should be prepared for objections from the outside world.
- In addition to acceptable reasons for removing an object, the museum must be legally allowed to do so.
- Deaccessioning should be an official and documented action of the board of trustees, based on the curatorial recommendations and information.

- Preapproved deaccessioning options should be noted in collection management policies previously approved by the board of trustees.
- All deaccession deliberations and approvals must be easily explained and recorded in hard copy for the museum's records.

Deaccession Ethics Controversy

Frequently, deaccessioning takes place without adverse repercussions. However, on occasion it can be quite controversial. In fact, it is still the one action a museum can take that causes vitriolic complaints, at least from a public relations standpoint. Adverse responses always cite a museum's ethical failures insofar as collection ownership commitment and preservation duties are concerned. Museums consistently promote their stewardship work insofar as getting and safely keeping collections is concerned. Deaccessioning marks a perceived ethical failure of this mission (appendix VII).

Museum profession guidelines call for the income from the sale of collections to be used for acquiring additional collections, or the direct conservation thereof. The loudest deaccessioning protests in the past few years have embroiled the Berkshire Museum in Pittsfield, Massachusetts. Its board of trustees decided to sell twenty-two artworks to raise funds and reorient the institution's mission away from art and toward science and history. Groups opposing the action declared that "it is considered unethical for an art institution to use the proceeds from the sale of art-works for anything other than acquisitions."[3]

Trustee-initiated deaccessioning can be a highly dubious exercise. These people are usually never qualified to fiddle with how the intellectual substance of a museum is realized in practice. They must be hands-off overseers, not hands-on manipulators. Naturally, they will at times have to make overarching institutional decisions that have a direct impact on collections, including their retention. Examples of this would include museums that have to close, merge, or change a mission.

Deaccession by Inter-museum Transfer: An Ethical Win-Win-Win-Win Option

A deaccession option increasingly seen as the most ethical collection removal choice is inter-museum transfer. This can be accomplished by sale or gift or a combination thereof. It is a win-win-win-win idea. When moved to another responsible institution, an item wins because it remains preserved. The museum removing the item wins by no longer having to care for it. The acquiring museum wins by responsibly expanding its collection. The public wins by still having access to the item for customary informational purposes. There are good examples to follow regarding inter-museum collection transfer. In recent years, two inter-museum deaccessions took place by major museums, the Brooklyn Museum in New York City and the Corcoran Gallery in Washington, DC, when it dissolved.

In 2008, it was announced that the Brooklyn Museum had agreed to divest itself of its large and excellent costume collection. It was transferred to the Metropolitan Museum of Art, which has an exceptional costume collection. The arrangement was heralded in an exhibition and lauded in the accompanying catalogue.[4] In 2018, the board of trustees of the Corcoran Gallery of Art in Washington, DC, decided to close the institution. In doing so, it elected to give the art collection to museums in the city (appendix VIII). The fact that neither decision resulted in collections vanishing in the commercial market and thus being kept preserved in the public sector is laudable.

Something given to a museum by a prominent person may be deemed worth keeping if only because of the notoriety of the donor. I am sure that was one reason the Museum of the City of New York found two other museums to take (presumably at their expense) two rooms from John D. Rockefeller's house on West 54th Street that had been on view at the museum for many decades. The Museum of the City of New York got rid of rooms that it did not want, the two museums receiving the rooms are happy, and the rooms will continue to be preserved.

Deaccession discussions sometimes suggest an unwanted gifted object be given back to the donor. This is unwise for several reasons, not the least of which may involve the Internal Revenue Service if the donor took a tax deduction for the value of the donation at the time it was gifted. It is impractical for items contributed so long ago that a donor cannot be located. And, what if two or more people made the gift but only one can be found? In the period room examples cited for the Museum of the City of New York, presumably no offers were made to members of the Rockefeller family about returning the rooms to them—whoever they might have been at the time.

Ethics debates regarding deaccessioning will rest on one or more of the following arguments:

- If the item being removed was a gift, donors, their heirs, or friends will be offended.
- The action will have an adverse impact on people's interest in making donations in the future.
- Unless transferred by sale or gift or some combination thereof to another qualified museum, the object will be lost to the public forever. Museum records will have little subsequent value.
- The work a museum devoted to protecting, studying, and/or caring for an item will have been for naught.
- The loss of one item jeopardizes all items in a museum's collection.

Involuntary Museum Collection Loss

Involuntary collection loss is the unplanned and unauthorized disappearance of an object from museum ownership. There are two variants of unanticipated museum collection losses: one is a consequence of internal factors and the other of external factors. Internal losses are caused by museum employees or operating system failures. External losses are generated by outside forces over which a museum may or may not have any control. In either case, losses are the result of human actions, inactions, or uncontrolled natural elements.

Collection Loss by Theft

There are various ways for how and why museum objects disappear. Theft tends to be the most common reason. Things are stolen from the owning museum or while outside the confines of the institution. The latter can happen when items are in transit or on loan to another museum. In addition to theft, losses can occur in the same places through human error or natural disaster. A staff member might drop an accessioned glass vase and shatter it beyond reconstruction. Delicate and already deteriorating early photographs can become lost because of poor storage. Vermin may consume historic textiles that are not rigorously protected. The ethics implications for these and similar collection assaults can be clear or murky. A staff member accused of employment errors or lapses can respond with a host of excuses, many involving the lack of funding to do his or her job "correctly." Given the lax and fluid nature of assigning positive behavioral expectations within the museum field, employees are rarely held accountable for lapses in judgment or dereliction of duty. If laws are broken though, legal action can be taken. Oddly, those measures tend to ignore ethics questions.

Stealing from museum collections is done by museum employees and people outside institutions. Frankly, I am amazed, but reassured, that internal theft does not happen more often. Collection managers are in the perfect position to walk off with things, as they can easily change records to help cover their tracks. For the most part, I believe most in the museum field are honest in our professional endeavors. It is unusual for internal thievery to happen. People close to collections hold high personal ethical standards. In the unlikely event a collection item is stolen by a museum staff member, the feeling of loss within an organization can be especially tragic. Theft by a colleague is disheartening. These are people you may work with closely or at least recognize distantly. Presumably, the assumption is they hold shared values when it comes to any altruistic commitment to their work. Given their museum employ, their transgressions are especially outrageous ethical violations.

Are there ethical implications when collections are lost to theft or destruction by human assaults and natural disaster? Are there ways to assess museum lapses that could be seen as violations of established positive safeguards? Starting with accountability, should anyone be held responsible? How is that determined? If individuals are the cause of losses are they from inside a museum, or outside, or both? Could the loss have been avoided? If so, how? What measures, physically and operationally, does or did a museum have in place to safeguard collections? Were there codes of ethics or perhaps generally agreed upon ethical precepts to support or even direct in some fashion ways to preserve collections from untoward loss? If so, in the case of a loss, were the protections followed? If not, why? These are just a few questions to be asked regarding involuntary collection losses. More may be added.

The majority of museum collection thefts, at least as reported in the media, are done by people outside museums. In the past few decades, the worst of these losses happened in 1990 when the Isabella Stewart Gardner Museum in Boston was robbed of thirteen artworks one night. The thieves were dressed as police and bamboozled the museum's night guards to let them in. No museum employees were held responsible for what was clearly a security training failure. Media alerts never touched on the ethics of the breach.[5]

When reported in the press, it seems the few examples of museum ethics violations involve non-collection-related scandals. In 2009, someone in the finance offices of the Brooklyn Museum was caught embezzling.[6] The most egregious theft over the past few years that was prosecuted to a stark conclusion involved the director of the Independence Seaport Museum in Philadelphia. John Carter was tried and convicted for the substantial use of museum resources for his own personal gain beyond his paycheck. He was sentenced to fifteen years in jail.[7] Fortunately, museum collection theft happens infrequently. There are probably two reasons for this: (1) museum security and the perceptions thereof are strong; and (2) the market for stolen museum collections is limited because losses are quickly made known to the public. Museum security has improved remarkably over the past several decades, largely as a result of improvements in both technology and training. Ethical concerns regarding collection security has meant fewer people have direct contact with objects, and when they do, their connectivity is usually restricted and monitored. There is much more sensitivity regarding who is authorized to work with collections and what that work will entail.

All museums should support or at least be aware of the Art Loss Register.[8] This organization lists, tracks, and helps in the retrieval of stolen art, artifacts, and specimens, be they taken from museums or private sector owners. While it seems museum collection loss involves obvious ethics lapses of some sort, that may or may not be the case. Reading about missing objects can tell volumes about good and bad behavior whether in the commercial market or in nefarious private transactions.

When I was a curator at the Museum of the City of New York, we had a very large ship model of an ocean liner named the SS *Majestic*. It was stolen while on loan to the South Street Seaport Museum in lower Manhattan. That museum was renovating the building the model was in. It was part of an exhibit of ship models. The renovation was taking place over the Christmas holidays. The museum was closed for several days. During that time, thieves broke into the gallery, which was on the ground floor, and made off with the model. The break-in was easily done. A back door that opened onto an inconspicuous alley had been removed by workmen. It was temporarily replaced by a sheet of plywood attached to the doorjamb by two nails. There was no operating security alarm system. Not until it reopened did the museum discover the removal of the plywood and the model loss. The museum's lack of adequate twenty-four-hour human and technological security and a failure to lock down the premises during the holiday closing were obvious security, not to mention ethical, breaches. At the time, the museum used a commercial independent security firm. Clearly, the company failed to attend to its duties. Whether this happened out of ignorance or as a result of absent or poor instruction from the museum was unknown.

Whether the theft of the *Majestic* was an "inside job" made possible with employee support or information is unknown. Given the size of the model (six-feet-long and contained in an even larger display case that was not taken), it was probably a planned robbery. No other models were taken. The Seaport Museum was embarrassed and apologetic, but no one was held responsible. The building renovators were not museum staff. It appeared they were neither instructed nor monitored regarding security measures. The model remains missing.

The case of a stolen ship model in no way approximates in magnitude or sorrow what happened at the Gardner Museum, but the outcomes are the same. Museum collection losses happened. Questions of ethics in both cases are similar. The lack of accountability is also similar. Regardless of one's job title and description, being aware of museum collection security is a shared duty. Certainly, some employees are more responsible for safety measures than others, but the current protective slogan often posted in public spaces holds true in museums: "If you see something, say something."

Collection Loss by Natural and Civil Disaster

When internal museum collection loss happens by natural disasters, including damage from light, fire, earthquake, or water, it might be the result of employee ignorance or lack of training. The most shocking recent example of fire loss occurred in 2018 when the National Museum of Brazil went up in flames.[9] The disaster was blamed on reduced government funding for the museum and especially the absence of a fire suppression system in the building.

Collection damage by water goes beyond simple flooding. Leaky roofs, broken water pipes, and rising dampness are a few ways water can get to and damage, if not totally destroy, collections. In addition, it is essential to recognize that humidity is a form of water, albeit not in its customary liquid nature. Materials react in various ways to high or low humidity and alarming fluctuations thereof.

Collection losses resulting from natural calamities generated outside museum boundaries would seem to excuse museums from ethics accountability. However, if an institution fails to take protective measures in anticipation of known potential calamities, fault may be found. Insurance companies will be ideal adjudicators in many instances. A museum located in a floodplain would do well to plan for inundations. Historic properties on rivers and oceanfront locations need to be especially careful of rising sea levels. Institutions in areas prone to forest fires, as happens in California often, should be watchful. This region is also subject to earthquakes. Predictions indicate these potential external natural threats to museums will only escalate with climate change. Ignoring qualified forecasts is a severe ethical lapse.

Museums would appear to be exempt from ethical blame for collection loss as a result of wars and civil disturbances. This is not always the case. Anticipating such upheavals can result in fortifying buildings or relocating collections to presumably safer locations. The latter option happened in Europe during the Second World War when the Louvre, among other museums, removed important art to be secretly kept elsewhere.

The list of collection catastrophes caused by war is very long. We might hope to protect museums from such murder and mayhem, but that is largely impossible. Sadly, even when a war is planned, safeguarding cultural treasures can be an afterthought, if a thought at all. The Iraq War in 2003 saw the devastation of the Iraq Museum in Baghdad. Thousands of objects were stolen, and much of the museum was damaged. No plans were devised to protect cultural sites in advance of the invasion.

Some consider museum collection losses during war possibly avoidable. They see the actions as ethical breaches of civilized behavior. Others simply shrug their shoulders and say war is hell. Museums might be fortunate to be protected during violent conflicts that unfold near or around them.

On a lighter note, sometimes an apparent collection loss is not. The Western Reserve Historical Society in Cleveland, Ohio, has a large collection of cars, and a few airplanes, in its Crawford Auto-Aviation Museum. One day years ago, when I was director of the society's museums, I came to work to find that five cars were missing from the large gallery. I was shocked and immediately sought an answer to this loss. It happened in February when there is an annual auto show in Cleveland. I was new at my job. No one had told me that every year a support group called the Friends of the Crawford Auto-Aviation Museum took collection cars to the show for a display to promote the museum. It was a homemade, do-it-yourself exhibit. While I was relieved that nothing criminal had happened, the arrangement was ethically questionable to say the least.

In Summary

Because most museum collections will remain where they are for the foreseeable future, ethics relating to all aspects of object acquisition, care, use, and occasionally disposal will adhere to generally accepted practices

ETHICS IN ACTION

1. A museum trustee offers to buy a collection object from the museum where he is a trustee. He has gotten an independent appraisal of the item's commercial worth. In addition to the proposed purchase price, he offers to also include a generous financial donation to the museum. What are the ethical ramifications of this request?
2. You are the director of a museum that has a large collection of photographs by a famous deceased American photographer. A well-known auction company is given several vintage prints to sell by a museum employee who has easy access to the collection cited above. This situation has been brought to your attention by another employee, who suspects foul play. What is an ethical approach to this situation?
3. The head of your museum's maintenance department has been repeatedly alerted by the collection manager about faulty roofing over the collection storage facility. He has made no effort to correct the situation or bring it to the attention of the director or board of trustees. When rain leaks, it is caught in buckets on the floor. These remain in place, rain or shine. What ethics concerns are there regarding this situation? If there are any, how should they be addressed? If there are none, why?
4. During a civil disturbance, a museum is broken into by a mob and many collection items are stolen. What would be an ethical way to respond to this event? What might be an unethical way to respond?

within the profession at large. Recognizing and accepting carefully crafted policy directives will accrue to the best interest of individual institutions, employees generally, and the material culture museums hold for the greater good. Fortunately, the two forms of museum collection loss outlined in this chapter pale when compared to the gargantuan nature of the totality of museum collections held in trust not only in the United States but around the globe. Given the importance of how ethical matters are determined and implemented insofar as collections are concerned, it will be wise for the profession at large to think about establishing a code of standards for all to follow. These should deal with all the aspects of collection acquisition, care, and use discussed here. Chapter 12 suggests an outline for approaching this idea.

Notes

1. Frank Rich, "And Now: 'Operation Iraqi Looting,'" *New York Times*, April 27, 2003, https://www.nytimes.com/2003/04/27/arts/and-now-operation-iraqi-looting .html.

2. A summary of deaccessioning can be found in Steven Miller, *Deaccessioning Today: Theory and Practice* (Lanham, MD: Rowman & Littlefield, 2018), 117.

3. "Activists Continue to Protest Berkshire Museum Art Sales," Artforum, July 3, 2018, https://www.artforum.com/news/activists-continue-to-protest-berkshire -museum-art-sales-75925.

4. Carol Vogel, "Brooklyn Museum's Costume Treasures Going to the Met," *New York Times*, December 15, 2008, www.nytimes.com/2008/12/16/arts/design/ 16muse.html.

5. Isabella Stewart Gardner Museum, "Gardner Museum Theft: An Active and Ongoing Investigation," https://www.gardnermuseum.org/organization/theft.

6. Dave Itzkoff, "Guilty Plea in Theft From Brooklyn Museum," *New York Times*, December 25, 2009, C2.

7. "Former Museum Lender Gets 15 Years for Fraud, Tax Evasion," *Philadelphia Business Journal*, November 2, 2007, https://www.bizjournals.com/Philadelphia/ stories/2007/10/29/daily42.html.

8. Art Loss Register, www.artloss.com.

9. Associated Press, "Fire Destroys Brazil's National Museum," NBC News, September 2, 2018; updated September 3, 2018, www.nbcnews.com/news/latin -america/firefighter-battle-massive-blaze-esteemed-rio-museum-n905901.

MUSEUM COLLECTION ETHICS STANDARDS

There is not one consistent set of standards that all companies follow, but each company has the right to develop the standards that are meaningful for their organization.[1]

Controlling Museum Collection Ethics

Today, like it or not, museums are subject to all sorts of collection ethics issues. As presented in this book, there are wide-ranging ownership and use debates, some well-known and others quite new. Stolen art has long embroiled museums in dispute. Today, even certain objects legally held are being claimed by individuals and groups outside the museum world. In addition, differing and vociferous opinions about exhibition content are increasing. Even acquisition practices are questioned. For instance, why are artists representing one ethnicity, gender, or race collected more than those of other demographic identities?

The chapters in this book outline philosophical and practical museum collection ethical concerns. They are arranged in a sequential manner, starting with how museums define themselves vis-à-vis collections. This is followed by looking at problems that can relate to the customary acquisition flow of objects as they enter museums, are cared for and used, and, even how some are removed from ownership. All these steps involve ethics questions. Prevalent ones have been noted, but peripheral questions will arise, and museums need to be ready to respond, often at a moment's notice.

How and what museums acquire tends to be a neutral subject insofar as the general public is concerned. However, as noted, there are exceptions that individuals take issue with. The idea of acquisition ethics is receiving increased attention. It is one of immense importance and will only grow. Museums need to set policies regarding what they collect, why, and how. How museums care for what they own was similarly a topic of little public concern. With the professionalization of the field, that has changed. Nonmuseum folks now understand there are proper and improper ways of dealing with museum collections. Since museums exist for public benefit, occasionally a member of that public (however defined) can accuse a museum of incompetence regarding the stewardship of its acquisitions. As museum exhibitions have become more open and welcoming to expanded audiences, criticisms can accompany accolades. These are usually presented as ethics complaints.

Ethics Standards

What some see as the subjective nature of ethics makes it difficult to establish an agreed upon canon of accepted characteristics—standards if you will. This is especially the case within the museum field. Regarding museum ethics and collections, what sort of standards should be established? The options are many. First, we need to define standards. A generic definition mentions excellence according to a commonly accepted model, or an approved consensus about actions and activities. This overarching characterization offers a good place to start. Who sets these agreed-upon points depends on the people and endeavors the standards are designed to help. Standards for police departments might not be the same as those for race car drivers—or for museums.

Since the advent of lengthy discussions about ethics in the museum profession, several groups have devised codes on the topic. They apply to the field generally or to specific aspects of it, such as curating or conservation. We hope they present the highest standards for whatever pursuit is being addressed. As is known, we increasingly rely on and insist upon having these codes in writing. This is a good thing. But, remember, as with a lot of written stuff, these documents are only as effective as they are worded, agreed to, monitored, and abided by.

"Any discussion of Codes of Ethics must recognize that such documents are in essence a series of value statements and principals that seek to represent a consensus view designed to guide individual behavior."[2] Ethics standards tend to be set and followed by two groups of participants—those who create them and those who abide by them. Given absent enforcement agreements, both the creators of museum ethics standards and those for whom the creations are intended play together when and if they wish. To my knowledge, no one has lost a museum job because of failing to devise a code of ethics and no one has lost a job because of any failure to abide by one.

What should museums do to operate at the highest ethical levels insofar as collections are concerned? They should set exemplary acquisition, ownership, and stewardship standards. These should be codified and approved by an institution's governing body. The standards should be annually reviewed and updated when evolving relevant ethics concerns dictate. The standards must be made known in full to employees and volunteers. Each must indicate agreement with the standards by signing a memo listing them fully. A standards document can be divided between what a museum will be responsible for and what employees and volunteers will be responsible for. The following offers an example:

THE XYZ MUSEUM COLLECTION STANDARDS

The XYZ Museum will have a formal written governance-approved collection policy that describes what it will collect to meet its mission. In addition to content regarding matters relating to quality, quantity, acquisition procedures, conservation, stewardship, and deaccessioning, the policy will include a listing of collection standards. As with all museum operating documents, these may be subject to change upon annual review. The standards will be available to the public in written and online forms. The standards will include the following elements.

- The Museum will:
  - Provide information in governance documents that explains the legal ownership role of the museum's collections.
  - Assure collections are acquired, cared for, and used in ways that directly reflect the institution's mission.
  - Have accurate and current collection records, especially for ownership and the transfer thereof to the institution be it by sale, gift, or a combination thereof.
  - Be certain museum staff <u>and volunteers</u> are aware of and know they have to abide by collection standards.
  - Set a schedule to review and update collection standards regularly.
  - Assure that the standards are contained in the personnel manual and referenced in governing documents.
  - Designate what positions are specifically responsible for museum collection acquisition, documentation, conservation, care, and use.
  - Assure timely access to profession advice, including legal counsel.
  - Support professional staff for designated procedures regarding any and all collection activities.
  - Be certain the standards are approved by the board of trustees.
- Museum employees and volunteers will:
  - Sign a copy of the collection standards agreeing to abide by them insofar as their job allows, and a copy of that document will be contained in the signing individual's personnel file.
  - Will not engage in personal or museum collection issues in any official capacity without preauthorization from designated museum authorities.
  - Avoid media when such involvement falls outside job duties.
  - Refer any and all research, media, use, or other collection inquiries to designated employees.

Ethics at Work

Museums are about truth; whose truth is a matter of opinion. Today, the truth aspect of museums is more socially respected than ever. This has little to do with anything new that these organizations do. They've been at it for a long time. The new popularity of museums has enhanced their credibility, though. This has been supported because other operations claiming certain truth-based missions are falling short on the veracity front. Schools, organized religions, and governments in particular have been found wanting as they fail to meet the high standards of content and conduct espoused by and expected of them. They are tinged with suspicion, ridicule, and scandal. While museums may occasionally succumb to content faults, for the most part they have avoided consistent or outrageous performance stumbles. This is the outcome of relentless definitional and operating diligence.

We would like ethics to be easily defined as positive or negative, black and white, moral or immoral, true or false, correct or incorrect, right and wrong. But, in the words of the old song, "it ain't necessarily so," while sometimes matters can be positive or negative, black and white, correct or incorrect, or right and wrong, all too often ethics depend on one's point of view. Further confusing the discussion, ethical ruminations can have nebulous outcomes: maybe, maybe not; who knows; beats me; or, it's a matter of opinion. Making the topic even more complex is its unpredictable fluidity. Actions considered perfectly ethical once upon a time (enslaving people, for example) are considered unethical now. To further confuse the issue, personal experience and perspectives too often play central roles in deciding ethics conduct. What I might feel is ethical, someone else might feel is unethical.

Those of us in the museum field may think that, for the most part, we are ethical people doing ethical things for ethical reasons every day and providing ethical environments for ourselves and the staff of our workplaces as well as those we serve. Based on my experience, this is usually true. However, regardless of how ethically conscious and conscientious museum staff and volunteers might be, in fact, we are not unbiased, unblemished, pure practitioners of a singularly truthful profession that is unaffected by the complications of a real, complex, and ceaselessly evolving world. On the job our motivations and endeavors regarding ethics are as subject to fungible considerations as is the case with any other human pursuit. Setting policies, monitoring adherence, and making alterations when advisable must be an ongoing museum governance and management occupation. Collections need to benefit from established ways of operating and must be secure when facing future changes.

Museums attract considerable attention. Most of it is positive. This is seen in good exhibit reviews, celebrations of new buildings and additions, and compliments about new staff appointments. But there are occasional complaints directed at museums. This book presents examples that either initially or ultimately revolve around ethics questions. What a museum might think is perfectly acceptable behavior others might take issue with.

In Summary

A museum's reputation is its most important asset. The singularity of that statement is actually a plural reality. How one museum behaves touches all museums. This is especially true regarding the only thing that makes museums unique—the real thing. Constant attention must be paid to

---

ETHICS IN ACTION

1. Your museum has been approached by the PBS television series *Antiques Roadshow* to host an episode. The format involves art and antiques dealers giving free monetary appraisals to members of the general public who bring items to be assessed. The show organizers want to locate the dealers throughout your museum, in its various galleries. Tables, easels, and display bases will be brought in for objects to be placed on while they are being discussed and appraised. The dealers will sit or stand by the items under discussion. The museum will receive a location fee and be featured in all publicity. The director will be interviewed on camera. What ethics concerns might the museum have regarding this request?

2. The small regional art museum that you direct has surveyed its collection and decided it contains too much art by straight white males and not enough by women, emerging artists, people of color, and anyone identified with the LGBTQ community. The board has decided to sell a large portion of the collection, including four pieces by a famous artist that will realize high prices on the market. What ethics issues might need to be understood and prepared for when following this plan?

3. A history museum is hiring a new curator. The successful applicant has a large personal collection of antique arms and munitions that directly parallel a collecting area of the museum. What ethics issues are involved with this hiring decision?

every aspect of collection acquisition, retention, preservation, and use. This requires meeting implied and actual declarations of responsibility to meet ethical behavior of the highest order. Fortunately, for the most part, most museums sustain this challenge but on occasion sins of omission and commission occur. An attentive awareness must infuse all museum collection operations and corrective action taken when warranted.

Going forward, concerns regarding museum ethics will only grow. There will be an expanded focus on collections in particular. Because museums are now a popular target for media attention in particular, how the things they own are treated will no longer be hidden in some academic Siberia. The idea that things have meaning and that meaning can vary widely according to an individual's, group's, tribe's, nation's, you-name-it's feelings, means museums must be constantly on guard when it comes to outside input about collection ownership and use. Opinions expressed will always be couched in ethics terms. Given the variability of ethics, as discussed in this book, there will be few absolute answers to questions museums must answer. Good Luck.

Notes

1. BusinessDictionary, "Ethical Standards," http://www.businessdictionary.com/definition/ethical-standards.html.

2. Marcelle Scott and Catherine Smith, "Ethics and Practice: Australian and New Zealand Conservation Contexts," in *Conservation Principles, Dilemmas and Uncomfortable Truths*, ed. Alison Richmond and Alison Bracker (London and New York, Routledge, 2009), 192.

APPENDIX I

MUSEUM POSITIONS WITH DIRECT COLLECTION CONNECTIVITY

There are a variety of positions at museums. Some, such as visitor services staff, have little or no direct physical contact with or intellectual oversight of collection decisions. Others, collection managers for instance, regularly interact with collections. Ethical concerns about how, when, why, or where employees connect with collections may not be noted in job descriptions, but they need to understand the subject. Institution codes of ethics are usually too general to include specific collection-concerned directives. Some jobs, such as conservation, have their own membership groups which may or may not have ethics protocols.

The following list provides standard titles and brief notations about how these jobs are or can be directly involved with museum collections. That involvement may be occasional, intermittent, or regular. Regardless, all must understand ethics ramifications of their actual or possible actions.

Director
Regardless of museum size, directors are ultimately responsible for what a museum acquires, how objects are spoken about on an official level, and how they are treated whether on view or behind the scenes. Directors must be key ethicists when it comes to the intellectual status of collections. Their impact ranges from acts of acquisition to ways of explaining them.

For the most part museum directors rarely interact with museum collections in any direct physical way. Few are qualified to handle collections carefully and thus such involvement could be questioned.

Curator
Curators are the principal subject and content specialists of museums. In that capacity they tend to be more familiar with collections than most other employees. Their ethical behavior toward collections must be above reproach always. In addition to assuring objects are appropriate to a museum, correctly acquired, and interpreted conscientiously, curators need to keep current with the changing ethical landscape of museum collection discussions.

Registrar or Collection Manager
The titles museum registrar and collection manager are given to staff responsible for museum collection record keeping and handling when objects are in storage or being moved. These employees are essentially the accountants for the collection. Some will know aspects of collections better than other museum personnel. As with curators, they must understand the role of ethical behavior when it comes to how collections are acquired, documented, stored, and handled. While the position does not require conservation knowledge, capabilities, or experience, it does call for a familiarity in this regard and when to consult experts. Because many ethical debates embroiling museums are about ownership, keeping and assuring accurate, full, and honest documentation of this is more important than ever. As with curators, it is important that registrars and collection managers keep current with museum ethics regarding collections.

Security
Poor museum collection security violates the trust museums establish by definition regarding the long-term care for the three-dimensional

documents they acquire and keep for public benefit. If a museum is at fault, failing to protect against theft, vandalism, and other assaults on collections is a gross ethical deficiency. Security employees need to be trained for customary surveillance and how to respond to emergencies. Perhaps the most alarming example of inadequate professional security coverage occurred in 1990 when thirteen works of art were stolen one night from the Isabella Stewart Gardner Museum in Boston. Nothing has been recovered and no museum personnel were held responsible. We know a museum has good security when nothing untoward happens.

Media Associate

Museums are places of communication and words obviously play a key role in that work. What words are used to explain activities, events, accomplishments, scholarship, etc. can have ethics consequences. Depending on the context and who is voicing a statement, referring to American Indians as Indians may be considered insulting. Commenting on a person's ethnicity as Oriental rather than Asian can cause offense. The language used in press releases, media alerts, or other public relations vehicles must be carefully applied. Staff in these positions need to be sensitive and always alert regarding what to say, how, when, and where.

Maintenance

There are occasions when maintenance staff interacts with museum collections, either when dealing with regular facility management or during emergencies. It is wise to train, or at least alert, these employees to the care collections require. This is especially true for sensitive materials. Assuring that nothing is handled that should not be by untrained individuals is particularly important and ethically sound procedure.

Exhibit Designer, Preparator, Installer

Museum employees responsible for and involved with exhibits interact with collections more than most staff. Though the interaction may be temporary and even brief, it is essential their actions are respectful and safe for whatever items they handle or impact. Questions regarding ethics will address how objects are shown, what display materials are used, and who comes in contact with collections. Exhibiting the work of living artists can require special considerations to comply with the maker's wishes.

Conservator

The conservation of collections embraces more ethical consider- ations than might be the case for any other museum activity. This is discussed at length elsewhere in this book and is well explained in appendix II. On a management and administrative level, institutions must be certain that people unqualified to go near collections stay away from them.

Retail Managers

Few people responsible for museum sales ventures interact directly with collections. However, they can make decisions about how col- lections are reproduced in myriad ways. The incredible variety of imagery appearing in all manner of applications is obvious when vis- iting any creative museum store. Questions relating to ethics include permissions to reproduce the art of living artists, using things already copyrighted, or deciding what parts of collections unencumbered by restrictions of any sort are appropriate to put on coffee mugs, scarves, key chains, wine glasses, etc. This can be especially sensitive when it comes to images of nudity.

Contract Employee

Museums hire all sorts of people to do all sorts of jobs. They can deal with maintenance issues, advertising campaigns, curatorial projects, computer needs. Some may come in contact with, or be near, collec- tions. Obviously, those circumstances require close monitoring by trained staff. However, decisions made by contractors can have eth- ical implications if not done with sense and sensitivity. For example, the work of consultants devising web pages must be approved well before the pages are implemented. Advertising campaigns must not insult or assault designated individuals or groups.

APPENDIX II

THE DECLARATION ON THE IMPORTANCE AND VALUE OF UNIVERSAL MUSEUMS, 2002

The international museum community shares the conviction that illegal traffic in archaeological, artistic, and ethnic objects must be firmly discouraged. We should, however, recognize that objects acquired in earlier times must be viewed in the light of different sensitivities and values, reflective of that earlier era. The objects and monumental works that were installed decades and even centuries ago in museums throughout Europe and America were acquired under conditions that are not comparable with current ones.

Over time, objects so acquired—whether by purchase, gift, or partage—have become part of the museums that have cared for them and, by extension, part of the heritage of the nations which house them. Today we are especially sensitive to the subject of a work's original context, but we should not lose sight of the fact that museums too provide a valid and valuable context for objects that were long ago displaced from their original source.

The universal admiration for ancient civilizations would not be so deeply established today were it not for the influence exercised by the artifacts of these cultures, widely available to an international public in major museums. Indeed, the sculpture of classical Greece, to take but one example, is an excellent illustration of this point and of the importance of public collecting. The centuries-long history of appreciation of Greek art began in antiquity, was renewed in Renaissance Italy, and subsequently spread through the rest of Europe and to the Americas. Its accession into the collections of public museums throughout the world marked the significance of Greek sculpture for mankind as a whole and its enduring value for the contemporary world. Moreover, the distinctly Greek aesthetic of these works appears all the more strongly as the result of their being seen and studied in direct proximity to products of other great civilizations.

Calls to repatriate objects that have belonged to museum collections for many years have become an important issue for museums. Although each case has to be judged individually, we should acknowledge that museums serve not just the citizens of one nation but the people of every nation. Museums are agents in the development of culture, whose mission is to foster knowledge by a continuous process of reinterpretation. Each object contributes to that process. To narrow the focus of museums whose collections are diverse and multifaceted would therefore be a disservice to all visitors.

Signed by the Directors of:
   The Art Institute of Chicago
   Bavarian State Museum, Munich (Alte Pinakothek,
   Neue Pinakothek)
   State Museums, Berlin
   Cleveland Museum of Art
   J. Paul Getty Museum, Los Angeles
   Solomon R. Guggenheim Museum, New York
   Los Angeles County Museum of Art
   Louvre Museum, Paris
   The Metropolitan Museum of Art, New York
   The Museum of Fine Arts, Boston

The Museum of Modern Art, New York
Opificio delle Pietre Dure, Florence
Philadelphia Museum of Art
Prado Museum, Madrid
Rijksmuseum, Amsterdam
State Hermitage Museum, St. Petersburg
Thyssen-Bornemisza Museum, Madrid
Whitney Museum of American Art, New York

APPENDIX III

A CODE OF ETHICS FOR CURATORS

AMERICAN ASSOCIATION OF MUSEUMS

CURATORS COMMITTEE, 2009

PREFACE

The Curators Committee of the American Association of Museums (CurCom) first developed *A Code of Ethics for Curators* in 1983 and revised the document in 1996. Recognizing that museums and museum work change over time and regularly present new concerns and challenges, CurCom established a work group in 2006 to review and update the *Code of Ethics*.

To establish standards and best practices for professional curatorial conduct and for the many curatorial functions at museums, the work group reviewed standards generally understood and accepted by museum associations and professional organizations throughout the world, including the Accreditation Commission and other AAM bodies. In addition, the work group invited national and regional museum associations and individuals currently engaged in curatorial work to comment on early drafts of the code.

Members of that work group and the authors of this document are: John Mayer, chair and curator, Maine Historical Society; James Burns, curator of history, Tempe Historical Museum; Stephanie Gaub, collections manager, Orange County Regional History Center; Brian H. Peterson, senior curator, James A. Michener Art Museum; and John Russick, senior curator, Chicago History Museum.

The Executive Committee of CurCom approved the final version of the *Code of Ethics for Curators* at the AAM Annual Meeting in 2009.

INTRODUCTION

The *Code of Ethics for Curators* describes the fundamental principles, core beliefs, and critical responsibilities that define curatorial work and provides guidelines for ethical conduct. Although intended specifically for museum curators, the *Code of Ethics for Curators* will benefit others in the museum field who may have different titles but perform functions similar or related to those of a curator.

CurCom recognizes that every museum operates with a unique set of resources. It encourages an open, balanced, and direct assessment of any area of conflict between an institution's practices and the principles described in this code.

[Note: For the purposes of this document, the word *object* is used consistently throughout to represent the full range of materials that may be part of any museum's collection, including but not limited to works of art, photographs, biological and geological specimens, anthropological artifacts, digital collections, oral histories, and archives and manuscript collections.]

I. ABOUT CURATORIAL WORK

Curatorial work is multifaceted. Depending on the institution, curators can be highly specialized experts with responsibilities in a particular collection area, or they can be generalists who control a broad range of materials and perform duties ranging from exhibition development to facility maintenance and usage.

Regardless of their situation, curators have distinctive responsibilities that focus upon: 1) the interpretation, study, care, and development of the collection, and 2) the materials, concepts, exhibitions, and other programs central to the identity of their museum. Because of their direct responsibilities for the collection and their role in the development of interpretive material, curators are ambassadors who represent their institution in the public sphere.

Curators understand not only their role within the museum but also the responsibilities of the governing board, administration, and other staff; and they respect the hierarchy of authority at their institution. They are responsible for providing leadership and expertise in a variety of areas within their museum and the larger museum community.

Curators fulfill a vital role in the ongoing process of improving and strengthening the practices of their museum. They advocate and participate in the development of institutional policies that reflect the principles contained in this *Code of Ethics*, and they work to resolve differences between existing institutional practices and established professional standards.

Public trust is earned and granted to museums by the people they serve, and is based on the idea that museums exist to serve the public and will act in the public's best interest. Curators recognize that meeting these obligations is essential to a museum's health and well-being. Therefore, curators do not limit themselves to following the letter of the law but also adopt and follow professional standards that reach beyond the law, including those outlined in this *Code of Ethics*. In doing so, they foster trust in the integrity of the curatorial profession and benefit their own museum, the community it serves, and museums in general.

II. DEFINITION OF A CURATOR

Curators are highly knowledgeable, experienced, or educated in a discipline relevant to the museum's purpose or mission. Curatorial roles and responsibilities vary widely within the museum community and within the museum itself, and may also be fulfilled by staff members with other titles.

Depending on their job duties, museum curators may do some or all of the following:

- Remain current in the scholarly developments within their field(s); conduct original research and develop new scholarship that contributes to the advancement of the body of knowledge within their field(s) and within the museum profession as a whole.

- Make recommendations for acquiring and deaccessioning objects in the museum collection.
- Assume responsibility for the overall care and development of the collection, which may include artifacts, fine art, specimens, historic structures, and intellectual property.
- Advocate for and participate in the formulation of institutional policies and procedures for the care of the collection that are based on accepted professional standards and best practices as defined by AAM, CurCom, and other relevant professional organizations.
- Perform research to identify materials in the collection and to document their history.
- Interpret the objects belonging or loaned to the museum.
- Develop and organize exhibitions.
- Contribute to programs and educational materials.
- Advocate and provide for public use of the collection.
- Develop or contribute to monographs, essays, research papers, and other products of original thought.
- Represent their institution in the media, at public gatherings, and at professional conferences and seminars.
- Remain current on all state, national, and international laws as they pertain to objects in the museum collection.

III. A CURATOR'S VALUES

Curatorial work is guided by the following values:

- **To serve the public good** by contributing to and promoting learning, inquiry, and dialogue, and by making the depth and breadth of human knowledge available to the public.
- **To serve the institution** by responsible stewardship of financial, material, and intellectual resources; by pursuit of the goals and mission of the institution with respect for the diversity of ideas, cultures, and beliefs; and by integrity of scholarly research.
- **To serve the museum profession** by promoting and practicing excellence, honesty, and transparency in all professional activities.

IV. CURATORIAL RESPONSIBILITIES

A. Research, Scholarship, and Integrity

Curators ensure the integrity and objectivity of their scholarship and research projects by compiling reference materials and supporting documentation, keeping abreast of current scholarship, and unfailingly acknowledging the scholarly and artistic contributions of others.

More specifically, curators must establish intellectual control of the collection under their care. They ensure that a record of each object in the collection is prepared at the time of acquisition and that the record and the object are systematically organized and retrievable. They conduct research on and record the provenance of all objects in or offered to the collection, and they are responsible for the accuracy of the documentation, whether prepared by themselves or others. Curators must be aware of all applicable national and international laws and never knowingly acquire stolen, illegally exported, or improperly collected objects.

B. Interpretation

Curators must commit themselves to developing the museum collection and interpretation of its objects with a respect for the needs of all potential patrons and in compliance with, but not restricted to, the standards for accessibility set forth in the Americans with Disabilities Act (ADA). Curators are responsible for ensuring that all verbal and written interpretation is accurate and accessible, physically and cognitively, whether prepared by themselves or their subordinates.

When preparing interpretive material, curators have a responsibility to an object's creator(s) and culture of origin. When possible and appropriate, they accurately and respectfully represent the creator's perspective, the object's historical and cultural context, and the object's history of use.

C. Acquisition, Care, and Disposal

Curators at collecting institutions should be guided by codes of ethics relating to their individual discipline and by international, national, and local laws affecting aspects of their responsibilities, including the acquisition and disposal of objects.

Curators develop the collection under their care in conjunction with the museum's stated mission and other institutional policies, procedures, and documents. They identify deficiencies in the collection, review potential acquisitions, and provide compelling reasons for adding objects to the collection in accordance with the acquisition policy of their institution. They thoroughly document new acquisitions and advocate the care of the collection according to accepted professional standards in their area of expertise.

Curators periodically review collection objects to assess the continued relevance of each object to the museum's mission. They refine the collection through judicious disposal of objects in accordance with the deaccession policy of their institution.

Deaccessioning is undertaken solely for the advancement of the museum's mission. Curators offer professional guidance and expertise to their museum's board of trustees or other governing authority to ensure that the museum does not suffer in any way as a result of the deaccessioning process. Deaccessioned objects are preferably offered for transfer to another cultural institution or for sale at a well-publicized public auction. Proceeds from the sale of collections may not be used for anything other than acquisition or direct care of collections. Any other use may create the appearance that the collection, which is held in public trust, is being sold to finance the operations of the museum.

In some cases, deaccessioned objects may be destroyed if the objects have deteriorated to the point that their research, interpretive, historical, or other value is compromised beyond reclamation; if they are slated for deaccessioning and no other repositories wish to acquire them; or if they contain toxins or other volatile components that place patrons, staff, or other collection objects at risk.

D. Collection Access and Use

Curators advocate and provide for public access to and use of the collection. Whenever possible, curators encourage and facilitate research inquiries, requests to examine objects, the use of objects in interpretive programs and exhibitions, and loans to other organizations—all in keeping with the institution's obligation of holding the collection in the public trust.

Curators recognize that the balance between preservation and use of collection objects is delicate. They discourage uses of the collection that may unnecessarily hasten the degradation or deterioration of any object.

When dealing with objects of cultural patrimony, including but not limited to human remains, sacred objects, and funerary objects, curators should consult with descendant communities regarding handling, storing, and exhibiting materials with consideration and respect for cultural traditions. When dealing with Native American collections, curators should ensure that their institution is in compliance with all Native American Graves Protection and Repatriation Act (NAGPRA) rules and regulations.

Awareness of and respect for donor restrictions and confidentiality, and respect for the object's creator(s) and cultural context, are paramount when considering requests for loans, access to objects, collection information, and any other use.

Curators offer professional guidance and expertise to their museum's board of trustees or other governing authority to ensure that the museum does not suffer in any way as the result of a loan of objects from the collection. Object loans should further interpretation and scholarship. Any other purpose may create the appearance that collection objects are being used for commercial or personal gain. Loans from the collection are granted following institutional policy.

Curators ensure that objects loaned to and from the museum receive at least the same care and protection as the objects under their care.

E. Replication of Objects in the Collection

Curators evaluate and support only those proposals to produce copies of collection objects for commercial or other purposes that guarantee the safety of an object and ensure that every copy will be accurate and that each use is in compliance with institutional policy. Any replication should be marked as a copy in a permanent manner and developed according to institutional policy. The replication of an object should in no way alter or devalue the original collection item.

V. CONFLICTS OF INTEREST

Museum staff and trustees regularly make decisions about what to collect, exhibit, study, and promote. The well-being of any museum depends on the public's confidence that its decision making is driven by the greater interests of the community it serves and is not unduly influenced by the potential for personal gain or the needs and practices of the marketplace. Curators respect the public purpose of museums and conduct themselves in a manner intended to protect both their institution and profession by putting the public interest first.

Often, when a conflict arises within an institution, it is the individual curator who is first aware of its existence and first to bring it to the attention of the museum's leadership. As curators and museums search for legitimate ways to resolve an ethical dilemma, it is essential that all parties work together for the benefit of the institution and the public it serves. The relationship between curators and institutions must be based on mutual trust and sound judgment.

A. General Statements

Curators are committed to the mission, goals, and policies of their institution, and they avoid conflicts of interest and the appearance of conflicts of interest. The perception of conflict of interest can be as damaging as an actual conflict; the public's trust of the entire museum profession is violated when the curatorial decision-making process is perceived to be influenced by a conflict of interest.

Curators often benefit personally and professionally from their association with a museum, enriching or advancing their careers through good work and through associations and contacts that are the normal result of curatorial activities. However, if curators use or appear to use their position with a museum purely for personal advantage or profit rather than in service of their institution and the public good, that behavior constitutes a conflict of interest.

Critical areas for potential conflicts of interest include personal collecting, dealing, gifts, outside employment, and consulting. In all pertinent areas, curators should assert leadership and advocate the creation of policies that define institutional expectations and standards of conduct. Written policies, which should be made available to all staff, help the museum establish and employ a consistent, evenhanded approach in all situations that involve a potential conflict of interest. If written policies do not exist, curators should seek the advice and consent of their supervisor until a policy is adopted.

B. Disclosure

Ethical decision making is rarely a matter of simply following preordained guidelines. Real-world situations are often complex; a thorough process of study and consideration typically precedes a decision about ethics. Openness and transparency are prudent, effective means of avoiding conflicts of interest and are essential conditions for the decision-making process.

Curators and guest curators should disclose potential conflicts of interest to their immediate supervisors in writing or by following established institutional policy.

C. Personal Collecting and Dealing

Curators often make or influence important decisions about the content of their institution's collection and exhibitions. The public good, not individual gain, is the primary concern in their decisions. Curators must not develop a personal collection that in any way compromises or is in conflict with the credibility or interests of their institution.

When curators build and maintain a personal collection in any area of interest that overlaps with their museum's identity and mission, a serious potential for an ethical conflict exists. For this reason, many institutions prohibit personal collecting by staff within the museum's mission; others allow it within closely prescribed guidelines.

Curators or guest curators may not be active dealers in the museum's areas of interest. Active dealers are individuals who have a registered business with commercial tax status or, more broadly, are actively engaged in the buying and selling of objects for personal or commercial profit. Guest curators are expected to operate within the same institutional guidelines that govern the behavior of staff curators in the areas of personal collecting and dealing.

D. Appraisals and Authentication

Curators who become involved in establishing the monetary value of objects or authenticating objects expose themselves and their institution to conflicts of interest and legal risks. Therefore, curators must not prepare appraisals for any reason. Curators should refer all interested parties directly to professional appraisers' societies or qualified appraisers. All referrals should be made without endorsement.

Curators may estimate insurance values for loans or other internal uses and should document the sources for these estimates. Some museums may allow curators to provide authentications under carefully controlled conditions per institutional policy.

E. Outside Employment

Outside employment includes situations in which curators who are principally employed by a museum also engage in work for an organization, an individual, or themselves on their own time and receive compensation for this activity. Some institutions prohibit outside employment; others allow it within closely prescribed guidelines.

Curators should conform to their museum's policy concerning outside employment and disclose any activity to their supervisor before accepting such responsibilities. In addition, curators must follow their institution's policies regarding lecture fees, royalties, and ownership of scholarly materials and copyrights. Curators, especially those who are also artists, need to be sensitive to the ethical issues that may arise in relationships with galleries, dealers, and professional colleagues.

F. Relationships with Vendors, Gifts

Personal relationships with vendors and other types of contributors may lead to or cause the appearance of favoritism and have legal and ethical ramifications. For this reason, gifts from vendors, collectors, or other parties who may be seeking influence or business with the museum may not be accepted. To avoid undue influence, curators and guest curators who have prior relationships with such parties should disclose those relationships to their supervisors.

As a result of their professional duties, curators may develop a personal relationship with a colleague, donor, associate, or artist. In such instances, personal gifts may be permissible in accordance with institutional policy.

Many institutions prohibit staff from accepting personal gifts; others allow it within closely prescribed guidelines. Gifts to the institution may be accepted by curators for their institution. If there is any question about appropriateness, curators should discuss the circumstances with their supervisor before accepting the gift.

AFTERWORD

This *Code of Ethics* is intended to be a living document—one that is regularly considered and continually improved. To that end, CurCom established a Standing Committee on Ethics with responsibility to review and update this *Code of Ethics* on a regular and ongoing schedule and to serve as a general resource for matters relating to curatorial ethics. CurCom's Standing Committee on Ethics is available to the curatorial field as a resource for information, discussion, and advice on ethical issues. Members of this committee can be contacted through www.CurCom.org.

SOURCES

The following documents were used as source material by the CurCom work group:

Publications

AAM Technical Information Service's Forum. *Writing a Museum Code of Ethics.* Washington, DC: AAM, 1994.

AAM Technical Information Center. "Standards and Best Practices for Museums." *Information Center Fact Sheet* (June 2007).

Edson, Gary. *Museum Ethics.* London: Routledge, 1997.

Eppich, Linda. "Ethics and the Museum Collection." *NEMA News* (Fall 2005): 2–3.

Philbrick, Harry. "Exhibition Ethics in the Non-collecting Museum: Looking Through the Other End of the Telescope and Finding Someone Looking Back." *NEMA News* (Fall 2005): 6–7.

Williams, Stephen L. "Critical Concepts Concerning Non-Living Collections." *Collections: A Journal for Museum and Archives Professionals* (August 2004): 37–66.

Sample Codes of Ethics

American Association of Museums. *A Code of Ethics for Museums.* Washington, DC: AAM, 2000.

American Institute for Conservation. *Code of Ethics and Guidelines of Practice.* 1994.

Museums Association (United Kingdom). *Code of Ethics for Museums*. 2002.

Usai, Paolo Cherci. "A Charter of Curatorial Values." *Journal of the National Film and Sound Archive* (Spring 2006): 1–10.

Jackie Weisz, comp. *Codes of Ethics and Practice of Interest to Museums*. AAM Technical Information Service. Washington, DC: AAM, 2000.

Reprinted with permission from the American Alliance of Museums.

APPENDIX IV

PENN MUSEUM STATEMENT ON HUMAN REMAINS

1.0 INTRODUCTION

This document has been developed by the University of Pennsylvania Museum of Archaeology and Anthropology (Penn Museum) to provide a clear statement about the respectful treatment and diligent curation of human remains in the Museum's care while supporting the Museum's commitment to understanding human biological and cultural variability around the world. Given the University's mission as a research and educational institution and the Museum's mission to transform understanding of the human experience through collections stewardship, research, teaching, and public engagement, the following statement provides a general framework that acknowledges the complexities of human remains as part of our collections and strives to ensure that any use of our collections is conducted in a professional and respectful way.

Research on human remains is at the core of the Museum's research agenda. It yields information on health, diet, population structure, and human interaction with the environment, as well as culture as seen, for example, in impacts on the human body, mortuary practices, social and political status, and inequality, all of which inform our understanding of human history and prehistory and contribute to our knowledge of living human population and cultural diversity.

Questions about this statement should be referred to the Director's Office (director@pennmuseum.org) of the Penn Museum. This statement will be subject to review as needed by the Museum's Human Remains Consultative Committee.

2.0 PRINCIPLES AND DEFINITIONS

This statement explicitly acknowledges that human remains are a special category of sensitive material. As such, our collections stewardship of human remains treats them with particular respect. The Museum recognizes that there are wide legal, ethical, and cross-cultural expectations and considerations that should be acknowledged with regard to the care and stewardship of human remains.

This statement is informed by the ethical codes promoted by various professional bodies such as the Association of American Museums (AAM) and the Society for American Archaeology (SAA). More specifically, the Museum is subject to NAGPRA (the Native American Graves Protection and Repatriation Act, Public Law 101-601) and related regulations and guidelines concerning Native American and Native Hawaiian remains.

For the purposes of this statement, human remains include tangible or recognizable bodies or parts of bodies of once living humans. They typically include bones and soft tissues where preserved, whether exposed or non-exposed to direct observation (e.g. wrapped mummies as an example of the latter), but potentially can include body parts that are naturally or culturally shed (e.g. teeth, hair, nails). Human remains can also form part of cultural objects (e.g. artifacts crafted directly out of human bone).

3.0 COLLECTIONS STEWARDSHIP

Since its founding in 1887, the Penn Museum has collected approximately one million objects, mostly obtained directly through its own field excavations and anthropological expeditions. The Museum's vast and varied collections are in active service to the University of Pennsylvania community and researchers around the world. They are housed in eleven (11) curatorial sections: African, American, Asian, Babylonian, Egyptian, European Archaeology, Historic, Mediterranean, Near East, Oceanian, and Physical Anthropology.

The Museum's human remains consist of more than 12,000 individuals from around the world and are curated primarily in the Physical Anthropology Section, with some exceptions found in the other Curatorial Sections. The Museum strives to adopt best practices for the stewardship and curation of human remains.

3.1 Documentation

The Museum's comprehensive inventory of its human remains is not currently publicly accessible. Questions about the inventory should be referred to the Physical Anthropology Section (physicalanthropology section@pennmuseum.org).

Human remains are described according to the best current scientific practices of physical anthropology. The data recorded include: identification numbers; culture area; cultural affiliation; period information; type of remains; age and sex; state or region of origin; location in state or region of origin; context in which remains were collected; collector or source of collection; collection date; status of location in museum; associated funerary objects, if applicable; and any additional information about the remains.

In addition, human remains are scientifically described with appropriate measurements. Approximately 700 measurements and observations can be made on a human skeleton depending on the completeness of the remains. These observations and measurements are essential to precisely identify the materials and are critical for our record keeping at the Museum.

Human remains are also documented by means of imagery. These images include standard black and white or color photographs as well as digital photographs. CT scans and radiology are also performed to provide basic documentation.

3.2 Acquisitions

The acquisition of human remains is handled on a case-by-case basis and generally derives from the transfer of remains from peer institutions (e.g.

the Academy of Natural Sciences of Drexel University) when the Penn Museum is deemed to be a more appropriate repository. All acquisitions are reviewed by the Museum's Acquisitions Committee in line with the Acquisitions Policy and Procedures. As of November 1990, the Museum acquires Native American human remains only in accordance with the provisions of Public Law 101-601.

3.3 Deaccessions

The deaccessioning of human remains is handled on a case-by-case basis and generally occurs as a result of NAGPRA-related repatriation processes overseen by the Museum's NAGPRA Committee. All deaccessions must be approved by the Trustees of the University of Pennsylvania.

3.4 Loans

The loaning or borrowing of human remains is handled on a case-by-case basis and generally occurs in response to specific requests for research or special exhibitions. The Registrar's Office handles all of the relevant processing in conjunction with the relevant Curatorial Sections. Borrowers are expected to conform to the principles outlined in this statement.

3.5 Storage

The Museum aspires to best practices for the collections stewardship and storage of human remains. Improvements are constantly being made in terms of storage containers, furniture, and environmental conditions.

3.6 Access

The Museum allows access to the human remains it stewards in line with its related missions of research, teaching, and public engagement. Access to collections storerooms is restricted to authorized staff, students, volunteers, and researchers, all of whom log their access in storeroom logbooks. Some special subsets of human remains (e.g. NAGPRA-related remains) are further restricted.

3.7 Handling

The handling of human remains is further restricted to those personnel who have undergone specific training. To facilitate our missions of teaching and public engagement, where handling human remains is less restricted for educational needs, the Museum has established special "teaching collections" of human remains.

3.8 Conservation

Human remains are sometimes stabilized using certain types of consolidants and adhesives. In general, when further conservation of human remains is required (e.g. to stabilize them for display), the Museum aspires to minimal intervention and the use of reversible treatments that will maintain the integrity of the remains.

3.9 Sampling

In some instances, sampling may be performed if it is determined by the Museum to be useful in the process of dating human remains, understanding population trends, and/or assigning cultural affiliation (e.g., 14C dating, isotopic analysis, DNA analysis). Requests for sampling are reviewed and approved by the Museum's Scientific Testing Committee. The sampling of any Native American or Native Hawaiian remains are also reviewed and approved by the Museum's NAGPRA Committee.

4.0 RESEARCH

Research on the Museum's human remains ranges from archival research that takes place in the Museum Archives to hands-on work that takes place within Museum storerooms to collaborative work around the world that uses samples derived from the Museum and to virtual research that makes use of the Museum's extensive collections of digital data (e.g. CT Scans, DNA data, and isotopic data).

Currently, the Museum does not have a comprehensive human remains research register that is publicly available, but interested parties should contact the Physical Anthropology Section (physicalanthropology section@pennmuseum.org) to inquire about past, current, and future research. For researchers who come to the Museum to work with human remains, they are expected to review our relevant research guidelines (e.g., Scientific Testing Policy and Procedures) and agree to them as needed.

5.0 DISPLAY

In some galleries, exhibitions, classrooms, publications, and online the Museum displays human remains and/or images of human remains respectfully in accordance with its overlapping missions of research, teaching, and public engagement. The Museum may choose to display human remains when their material component is deemed necessary for the interpretation of understandings of the human experience.

The Museum informs visitors about the display of recognizable human remains in its exhibition spaces. Since much of the Museum's exhibition galleries are also corridors thru the Museum, the Exhibition Team considers the location of human remains on display carefully and provides explanatory labels or materials to interpret the human remains for visitors.

6.0 EDUCATIONAL USE

The Museum may choose to use human remains for educational purposes, primarily through guided tours of gallery displays, when they are deemed necessary for the interpretation of anthropological or archaeological understandings of the human experience. The Museum's educational use of human remains includes University-level teaching and educational programs designed for middle school, high school, and adult audiences.

6.1 University teaching

An essential component of the Museum's teaching mission is to train undergraduates and graduate students in anthropology and archaeology. Understanding the nature and significance of human remains, is essential when studying human evolution, anatomy, growth & development, and forensics. Although replicas of hominid fossils are key tools for elucidating human evolution, nothing compares to the reality of actual human remains when trying to understand the range and variation of anthropological, biological, and physical traits and characteristics. As a result, the Museum's teaching collections and curated human remains form an active component of undergraduate and graduate-level training.

6.2 Public programs

The Museum's Public Programs Department on occasion hosts programs that involve or pertain to human remains. In appropriate instances, and under the supervision of appropriate personnel who facilitate the interaction with visitors, the Museum may choose to display human remains respectfully in accordance with our overlapping missions of research, teaching, and public engagement.

6.3 K-12 teaching

The Museum's Learning Programs Department which focuses mainly on K-12 audiences and K-12 teachers, does not use human remains in their museum educator-facilitated teaching or programs. Replicas are substituted where needed. Upon request, some special K-12 programs about forensic science using human remains are facilitated by Physical Anthropology specialists.

6.4 Special curricular training

In rare circumstances, human remains are used by personnel in the Physical Anthropology Section to fulfill special curricular needs of non-university students (e.g., community service programs, internships, and tours).

Reproduced with permission of the Penn Museum—University of Pennsylvania Museum of Archeology and Anthropology. The statement is available at https://www.penn.museum/about-collections/statements-and-policies/human-remains.

APPENDIX V

THE CLEVELAND MUSEUM OF ART NEWS RELEASE ON OPEN ACCESS

News Release
FOR IMMEDIATE RELEASE
Wednesday, January 23, 2019
Kelley Notaro Schreiber
The Cleveland Museum of Art
knotaro@clevelandart.org
216-707-6898

Brings museum's mission "for the benefit of all the people forever" into the digital age

Cleveland, OH (January 23, 2019)—The Cleveland Museum of Art (CMA) announced today it is using Open Access to make high-resolution digital images and collections data freely available by means of the internet. Open Access means the public now has the ability to share, remix, and reuse images of as many as 30,000 CMA artworks that are in the public domain for commercial as well as scholarly and noncommercial purposes. Additional information on more than 61,000 artworks—both those in the public domain and those with copyright or other restrictions—is also now available.

"The CMA's Open Access program brings our mission 'for the benefit of all the people forever' into the digital age," said William Griswold, director. "With Open Access, the museum makes its collection of art from all periods and parts of the world easier to access and more relevant to the public. As a global leader among museums, the CMA is committed to transparency and universal access, and we anticipate that other institutions around the world will undertake similar initiatives in order to engage new audiences and help bring art to life for all."

The CMA's Open Access program is the most comprehensive to date, with high-resolution images in both JPG and TIF formats as well as a fully operable application programming interface (API) that can be accessed at http://openaccess-api.clevelandart.org/ [1]. Among the significant features of the CMA's Open Access offering are rich metadata with the inclusion of authored text, exhibition history, bibliographic citations, catalogue raisonné numbers, and provenance information for each artwork. Collection data in both the CSV and JSON file formats can be accessed via a GitHub repository at https://github.com/ClevelandMuseumArt/openaccess [2].

Chief Digital Information Officer Jane Alexander explained, "The Cleveland Museum of Art's Open Access program builds on its reputation for innovative digital projects including the ARTLENS Gallery. With its world-class collection and talented team, we are able to launch with a robust, usable toolset that will inspire artists, creative developers, and communities to leverage our expansive and comprehensive dataset."

The CEO of Creative Commons, Ryan Merkley, said, "Creative Commons Search Beta, the open online search and reuse tool that allows high-quality content from the Commons to surface in a seamless and accessible way, now includes as many as 30,000 CMA images under CC0 designation. The goal of Creative Commons is to help institutions and individuals legally share knowledge and creativity to build a more equitable, accessible, and innovative world."

In conjunction with this new initiative, the museum is launching its newly redesigned online collection to make it easy for individuals, scholars, students, and virtual visitors to have access to a wealth of information on art. This includes up to 35 fields of metadata with descriptive text, creating more possibilities for semantic relationships, contextual interpretations, and translations related to artworks in the collection. In addition, the museum's website will allow visitors to choose the view that is best for them, whether it's text-heavy or image-focused. The CMA has also added a refined advanced search to make finding artworks simple and intuitive. This improved feature is powered by Microsoft's Azure search-as-a-service cloud solution and will enable users to search by specific fields, providing art historians and enthusiasts alike an opportunity to dive deeper into the collection. A newly incorporated elastic search improves the accuracy of results, including the ability to sort more easily. An auto-complete search bar proposes potential searches and suggests correct spellings for artist names.

Kate D'Orazio, Product Marketing Manager at AI Platform, Microsoft, said, "One of our core values at Microsoft is to make the world more accessible, which is why we wanted to make it possible for more people to see and explore art. We are excited to be part of this milestone for public access to the art and humanities. Thanks to the new AI capabilities within Azure Search, the public can explore and understand the CMA's outstanding collection better than ever before."

In addition to Creative Commons, Wikimedia, Internet Archive, Artstor, and Artsy have incorporated the CMA's public domain collection into their websites, thus increasing the view of CMA images around the world and in multiple languages. Because of the museum's application programming interface (API), these sites will update regularly with new content from the CMA.

Along with its new Open Access digital policy, the CMA allows the visiting public to capture its own still and moving images of the museum's artworks that are in the public domain and on public display with handheld devices for commercial and noncommercial purposes, provided there is no disruption to museum operations or guest accessibility. The CMA waives rights to media created by users capturing public-domain artworks in its collections and even encourages the public to consider contributing the works they create from its collections with Creative Commons legal tools to the Commons of shared cultural heritage. This policy update is in coordination with the CMA's own contribution of images and data to the public domain with its Open Access initiative policy: http://www.clevelandart.org/visit/visitor-information/museum-policies [3].

Visit the CMA's collection online to research, study, and download Open Access images: http://www.clevelandart.org/art/collection/search [4].

The CMA acknowledges the Metropolitan Museum of Art (United States), Walters Art Museum (United States), the Rijksmuseum (The Netherlands), Cooper-Hewitt, Smithsonian Design Museum (United States), and the Statens Museum for Kunst (Denmark) for their foundational work with Open Access and use of Creative Commons Zero to share public domain images and data with the public.

At launch, leading national and international organizations will provide demonstrable examples of the benefits of Open Access, magnifying the initiative's impact and reach beyond the CMA's own website and subdomains. Content partners for the launch are American Greetings, Artstor, Artsy, Case Western Reserve University, Creative Commons, Europeana, Hyland Software, Internet Archive, Microsoft Corporation, Pandata, and Wikimedia.

The event and initiative are sponsored by MCPc, BlueBridge Networks, and Kevin and Tracy Goodman. Neal Stimler, senior advisor at Balboa Park Online Collaborative, supported the CMA with its Open Access initiative as a consultant.

Refer to the museum's Open Access page, clevelandart.org/open-access [5], for details about the initiative and partnership activities.

* * *

About the Cleveland Museum of Art

The Cleveland Museum of Art is renowned for the quality and breadth of its collection, which includes more than 61,000 objects and spans 6,000 years of achievement in the arts. The museum is a significant international forum for exhibitions, scholarship, and performing arts. One of the top comprehensive art museums in the nation and free of charge to all, the Cleveland Museum of Art is located in the dynamic University Circle neighborhood.

The Cleveland Museum of Art is supported by a broad range of individuals, foundations and businesses in Cleveland and Northeast Ohio. The museum is generously funded by Cuyahoga County residents through Cuyahoga Arts and Culture. Additional support comes from the Ohio Arts Council, which helps fund the museum with state tax dollars to encourage economic growth, educational excellence and cultural enrichment for all Ohioans. For more information about the museum, its holdings, programs and events, call 888-CMA-0033 or visit ClevelandArt.org.

APPENDIX VI

AMERICAN INSTITUTE FOR CONSERVATION OF HISTORIC AND ARTISTIC WORKS

CORE DOCUMENTS: *CODE OF ETHICS AND GUIDELINES FOR PRACTICE*

HISTORICAL BACKGROUND

Code of Ethics and Guidelines for Practice; Commentaries

The first formulation of standards of practice and professional relations by any group of art conservators was produced by the IIC-American Group (now AIC) Committee on Professional Standards and Procedures. Formed at the second regular meeting of the IIC-AG, in Detroit, May 23, 1961, the committee worked under the direction of Murray Pease, conservator, Metropolitan Museum of Art; other members of the committee were Henri H. Courtais, Dudley T. Easby, Rutherford J. Gettens, and Sheldon Keck. The Report of the Murray Pease Committee: IIC American Group Standards of Practice and Professional Relations for Conservators was adopted by the IIC-AG at the 4th annual meeting in New York on June 8, 1963. It was published in *Studies in Conservation* in August 1964, 9(3): 116–21. The primary purpose of this document was: "to provide accepted criteria against which a specific procedure or operation can be measured when a question as to its adequacy has been raised."

The first formulation of a code of ethics for art conservators was adopted by the members of IIC-American Group at the annual meeting in Ottawa, Ontario, Canada, on May 27, 1967. It was produced by the Committee on Professional Relations: Sheldon Keck, chair; Richard D. Buck; Dudley T. Easby; Rutherford J. Gettens; Caroline Keck; Peter Michaels; and Louis Pomerantz. The primary purpose of this document was: "to express those principles and practices which will guide the art conservator in the ethical practice of his profession."

These two documents, *The Murray Pease Report: Standards of Practice and Professional Relationships for Conservators* and the *Code of Ethics for Art Conservators* were published in booklet form by the IIC-AG in May 1968 together with the Articles of Association of IIC and Bylaws of the American Group.

In 1977, the Ethics and Standards Committee (Elisabeth C. G. Packard, chair; Barbara H. Beardsley; Perry C. Huston; Kate C. Lefferts; Robert M. Organ; and Clements L. Robertson) was charged with updating the two documents to reflect changes in the profession. The 1968 format was retained, except that the more general *Code of Ethics* was placed first as Part One, followed by the *Standards of Practice* as Part Two. These revised versions of the code and standards were approved by the Fellows of AIC on May 31, 1979, at the annual meeting in Toronto. This document was amended on May 24, 1985, at the annual meeting in Washington, DC, to reflect the addition to the AIC Bylaws of procedures for the reporting, investigation, and review of alleged violations of the code and standards and of mechanisms for appealing such allegations.

Between 1984 and 1990 the Ethics and Standards Committee, responding to further growth and change in the profession, and following several years of AIC discussion on the issue of certification, was charged by the AIC Board to work on more substantial revisions of the document. This was done by soliciting commentary from the specialty groups and also from the membership via issues sessions at the annual meetings in Chicago (1986) and Cincinnati (1989). Following this, a document consisting of a new simplified *Code*, prepared by the committee, and a revised *Standards*, prepared primarily by the board, was presented to the membership for discussion at the 1990 annual meeting in Richmond. The consensus of the membership at the meeting was to continue the revision process. During these important years, the members of the committee were: Elisabeth Batchelor, chair; Robert Futernick; Meg Loew Craft (until 1989); Elizabeth Lunning (from 1987); Carol C. Mancusi-Ungaro; and Philip Vance (until 1986). In 1989, the committee added corresponding members Barbara Appelbaum, Paul N. Banks, Steven Prins, and Elisabeth West FitzHugh.

In 1990, the AIC Board charged a newly appointed committee to assess the role and use of the two parts of the *Code of Ethics and Standards for Practice* and as well to analyze specific difficulties within them. The committee first undertook an in-depth comparative analysis of the two sections, organizing them topically and relating them to other codes of ethics both in conservation and in other professions. Between September 1991 and May 1992, the committee produced five lengthy discussion papers on basic issues as supplements to the *AIC News* (prior to November 1991, the *AIC Newsletter*).

From these papers, the committee compiled an extensive body of commentary from the membership and specialty groups, supplementing that obtained previously. It then began the creation of a new revision of the entire document, the first draft of which was published in the September 1993 *AIC News* following a discussion session at the 1993 annual meeting in Denver. A revised draft was published in the May 1994 *AIC News* and discussed at the 1994 annual meeting in Nashville.

The final version of the document, consisting of a new simplified *Code of Ethics* and the creation of *Guidelines for Practice* to replace the *Standards of Practice*, was prepared and approved by AIC Fellows and Professional Associates through a mail vote in August 1994. The goals and purposes of the committee and the problematic issues it sought to address in creating the revised document are fully described in the committee's columns in the September 1991 *AIC Newsletter* and September 1993 *AIC News*.

Ethics and Standards Committee members from 1990 through 1994 and involved in the creation of the revised *Code and Guidelines* were: Debbie Hess Norris (chair, resigned 1993); Donna K. Strahan (co-chair 1993–94, chair 1994); Carol Aiken (co-chair from 1993, resigned 1994); Nancy Ash; Dan Kushel; Robert Espinosa (from 1993); and Paul Himmelstein (from 1994).

Commentaries

An integral part of the revision plan was also to initiate the creation of a second document, *Commentaries to the Guidelines for Practice*, upon final approval of the *Code and Guidelines*. Proposed to the committee by then AIC President Paul Himmelstein, this document was designed to amplify and define current accepted practice for each of the *Guidelines* while accommodating the individual needs of each area of professional specialization, and as well, allowing for future growth and change in practice through a simplified amendment process. Among core documents of professional conservation organizations, the AIC *Commentaries* are unique.

The creation of the *Commentaries* began in 1995, with full involvement of all AIC Specialty Groups and the Ethics and Standards Committee. The working process is fully described in the March 1995 *AIC News*. A Commentaries Task Force chaired by Paul Himmelstein was created in 1999 to further facilitate the process. The first *Commentaries* (24–28 on documentation) were approved by the Board in 1996. The final *Commentaries*, completing the set for all twenty-nine *Guidelines*, were finished in 2000 and approved by the AIC Board in May 2001.

Major revisions of *Commentaries* 24 and 28, to accommodate the transition to digital documentation in conservation practice, were developed by the AIC Digital Photographic Documentation Task Force chaired by Jeffrey Warda and were approved by the AIC Board in 2008. A detailed discussion of these revisions appears in Jeffrey Warda, ed., *The AIC Guide to Photography and Conservation Documentation*, Second Edition, 2011, chapter 5, part 6.

- Historical background prepared by: Elisabeth C. G. Packard, Chair, Ethics and Standards Committee 1977–1979. Amended May 24, 1985
- Revised August 1994; Revised and amended February 2015, Dan Kushel, member (1990–1994) and Chair, Ethics and Standards Committee 1995–1996

PREAMBLE

The primary goal of conservation professionals, individuals with extensive training and special expertise, is the preservation of cultural property.

Cultural property consists of individual objects, structures, or aggregate collections. It is material which has significance that may be artistic, historical, scientific, religious, or social, and it is an invaluable and irreplaceable legacy that must be preserved for future generations.

In striving to achieve this goal, conservation professionals assume certain obligations to the cultural property, to its owners and custodians, to the conservation profession, and to society as a whole. This document, the *Code of Ethics and Guidelines for Practice* of the American Institute for Conservation of Historic & Artistic Works (AIC), sets forth the principles that guide conservation professionals and others who are involved in the care of cultural property.

CODE OF ETHICS OF THE AMERICAN INSTITUTE FOR CONSERVATION OF HISTORIC & ARTISTIC WORKS

I. The conservation professional shall strive to attain the highest possible standards in all aspects of conservation, including, but not limited to, preventive conservation, examination, documentation, treatment, research, and education.

II. All actions of the conservation professional must be governed by an informed respect for the cultural property, its unique character and significance, and the people or person who created it.

III. While recognizing the right of society to make appropriate and respectful use of cultural property, the conservation professional shall serve as an advocate for the preservation of cultural property.

IV. The conservation professional shall practice within the limits of personal competence and education as well as within the limits of the available facilities.

V. While circumstances may limit the resources allocated to a particular situation, the quality of work that the conservation professional performs shall not be compromised.

VI. The conservation professional must strive to select methods and materials that, to the best of current knowledge, do not adversely affect cultural property or its future examination, scientific investigation, treatment, or function.

VII. The conservation professional shall document examination, scientific investigation, and treatment by creating permanent records and reports.

VIII. The conservation professional shall recognize a responsibility for preventive conservation by endeavoring to limit damage or deterioration to cultural property, providing guidelines for continuing use and care, recommending appropriate environmental conditions for storage and exhibition, and encouraging proper procedures for handling, packing, and transport.

IX. The conservation professional shall act with honesty and respect in all professional relationships, seek to ensure the rights and opportunities of all individuals in the profession, and recognize the specialized knowledge of others.

X. The conservation professional shall contribute to the evolution and growth of the profession, a field of study that encompasses the liberal arts and the natural sciences. This contribution may be made by such means as continuing development of personal skills and knowledge, sharing of information and experience with colleagues, adding to the profession's written body of knowledge, and providing and promoting educational opportunities in the field.

XI. The conservation professional shall promote an awareness and understanding of conservation through open communication with allied professionals and the public.

XII. The conservation professional shall practice in a manner that minimizes personal risks and hazards to co-workers, the public, and the environment.

XIII. Each conservation professional has an obligation to promote understanding of and adherence to this Code of Ethics.

The conservation professional should use the following *Guidelines* and supplemental *Commentaries* together with the AIC *Code of Ethics* in the pursuit of ethical practice. The *Commentaries* are separate documents, created by the AIC membership, that are intended to amplify this document and to accommodate growth and change in the field.

GUIDELINES FOR PRACTICE OF THE AMERICAN INSTITUTE FOR CONSERVATION OF HISTORIC & ARTISTIC WORKS

PROFESSIONAL CONDUCT

1. **Conduct:** Adherence to the *Code of Ethics and Guidelines for Practice* is a matter of personal responsibility. The conservation professional should always be guided by the intent of this document, recognizing that specific circumstances may legitimately affect professional decisions.

2. **Disclosure:** In professional relationships, the conservation professional should share complete and accurate information relating to the efficacy and value of materials and procedures. In seeking and disclosing such information, and that relating to analysis and research, the conservation professional should recognize the importance of published information that has undergone formal peer review.

3. **Laws and Regulations:** The conservation professional should be cognizant of laws and regulations that may have a bearing on professional activity. Among these laws and regulations are those concerning the rights of artists and their estates, occupational health and safety, sacred and religious material, excavated objects, endangered species, human remains, and stolen property.

4. **Practice:** Regardless of the nature of employment, the conservation professional should follow appropriate standards for safety, security, contracts, fees, and advertising.

4a. **Health and Safety:** The conservation professional should be aware of issues concerning the safety of materials and procedures and should make this information available to others, as appropriate.

4b. **Security:** The conservation professional should provide working and storage conditions designed to protect cultural property.

4c. **Contracts:** The conservation professional may enter into contractual agreements with individuals, institutions, businesses, or government agencies provided that such agreements do not conflict with principles of the *Code of Ethics and Guidelines for Practice*.

4d. **Fees:** Fees charged by the conservation professional should be commensurate with services rendered. The division of a fee is acceptable only when based on the division of service or responsibility.

4e. **Advertising:** Advertising and other representations by the conservation professional should present an accurate description of credentials and services. Limitations concerning the use of the AIC name or membership status should be followed as stated in the AIC Bylaws, section II, 13.

5. **Communication:** Communication between the conservation professional and the owner, custodian, or authorized agent of the cultural property is essential to ensure an agreement that reflects shared decisions and realistic expectations.

6. **Consent:** The conservation professional should act only with the consent of the owner, custodian, or authorized agent. The owner, custodian, or agent should be informed of any circumstances that necessitate significant deviations from the agreement. When possible, notification should be made before such changes are made.

7. **Confidentiality:** Except as provided in the *Code of Ethics and Guidelines for Practice*, the conservation professional should consider relationships with an owner, custodian, or authorized agent as confidential. Information derived from examination, scientific investigation, or treatment of the cultural property should not be published or otherwise made public without written permission.

8. **Supervision:** The conservation professional is responsible for work delegated to other professionals, students, interns, volunteers, subordinates, or agents and assignees. Work should not be delegated or

subcontracted unless the conservation professional can supervise the work directly, can ensure proper supervision, or has sufficient knowledge of the practitioner to be confident of the quality of the work. When appropriate, the owner, custodian, or agent should be informed if such delegation is to occur.

9. **Education:** Within the limits of knowledge, ability, time, and facilities, the conservation professional is encouraged to become involved in the education of conservation personnel. The objectives and obligations of the parties shall be agreed upon mutually.

10. **Consultation:** Since no individual can be expert in every aspect of conservation, it may be appropriate to consult with colleagues or, in some instances, to refer the owner, custodian, or authorized agent to a professional who is more experienced or better equipped to accomplish the required work. If the owner requests a second opinion, this request must be respected.

11. **Recommendations and References:** The conservation professional should not provide recommendations without direct knowledge of a colleague's competence and experience. Any reference to the work of others must be based on facts and personal knowledge rather than on hearsay.

12. **Adverse Commentary:** A conservation professional may be required to testify in legal, regulatory, or administrative proceedings concerning allegations of unethical conduct. Testimony concerning such matters should be given at these proceedings or in connection with paragraph 13 of these *Guidelines*.

13. **Misconduct:** Allegations of unethical conduct should be reported in writing to the AIC president as described in the AIC Bylaws, section II, 12. As stated in the bylaws, all correspondence regarding alleged unethical conduct shall be held in the strictest confidence. Violations of the *Code* and *Guidelines* that constitute unethical conduct may result in disciplinary action.

14. **Conflict of Interest:** The conservation professional should avoid situations in which there is a potential for a conflict of interest that may

affect the quality of work, lead to the dissemination of false information, or give the appearance of impropriety.

15. **Related Professional Activities:** The conservation professional should be especially mindful of the considerable potential for conflict of interest in activities such as authentication, appraisal, or art dealing.

EXAMINATION AND SCIENTIFIC INVESTIGATION

16. **Justification:** Careful examination of cultural property forms the basis for all future action by the conservation professional. Before undertaking any examination or tests that may cause change to cultural property, the conservation professional should establish the necessity for such procedures.

17. **Sampling and Testing:** Prior consent must be obtained from the owner, custodian, or agent before any material is removed from a cultural property. Only the minimum required should be removed, and a record of removal must be made. When appropriate, the material removed should be retained.

18. **Interpretation:** Declarations of age, origin, or authenticity should be made only when based on sound evidence.

19. **Scientific Investigation:** The conservation professional should follow accepted scientific standards and research protocols.

PREVENTIVE CONSERVATION

20. **Preventive Conservation:** The conservation professional should recognize the critical importance of preventive conservation as the most effective means of promoting the long-term preservation of cultural property. The conservation professional should provide guidelines for continuing use and care, recommend appropriate environmental conditions for storage and exhibition, and encourage proper procedures for handling, packing, and transport.

TREATMENT

21. **Suitability:** The conservation professional performs within a continuum of care and will rarely be the last entrusted with the conservation of a cultural property. The conservation professional should only recommend or undertake treatment that is judged suitable to the preservation of the aesthetic, conceptual, and physical characteristics of the cultural property. When nonintervention best serves to promote the preservation of the cultural property, it may be appropriate to recommend that no treatment be performed.

22. **Materials and Methods:** The conservation professional is responsible for choosing materials and methods appropriate to the objectives of each specific treatment and consistent with currently accepted practice. The advantages of the materials and methods chosen must be balanced against their potential adverse effects on future examination, scientific investigation, treatment, and function.

23. **Compensation for Loss:** Any intervention to compensate for loss should be documented in treatment records and reports and should be detectable by common examination methods. Such compensation should be reversible and should not falsely modify the known aesthetic, conceptual, and physical characteristics of the cultural property, especially by removing or obscuring original material.

DOCUMENTATION

24. **Documentation:** The conservation professional has an obligation to produce and maintain accurate, complete, and permanent records of examination, sampling, scientific investigation, and treatment. When appropriate, the records should be both written and pictorial. The kind and extent of documentation may vary according to the circumstances, the nature of the object, or whether an individual object or a collection is to be documented. The purposes of such documentation are:

- to establish the condition of cultural property;
- to aid in the care of cultural property by providing information helpful to future treatment and by adding to the profession's body of knowledge;

- to aid the owner, custodian, or authorized agent and society as a whole in the appreciation and use of cultural property by increasing understanding of an object's aesthetic, conceptual, and physical characteristics; and
- to aid the conservation professional by providing a reference that can assist in the continued development of knowledge and by supplying records that can help avoid misunderstanding and unnecessary litigation.

25. **Documentation of Examination:** Before any intervention, the conservation professional should make a thorough examination of the cultural property and create appropriate records. These records and the reports derived from them must identify the cultural property and include the date of examination and the name of the examiner. They also should include, as appropriate, a description of structure, materials, condition, and pertinent history.

26. **Treatment Plan:** Following examination and before treatment, the conservation professional should prepare a plan describing the course of treatment. This plan should also include the justification for and the objectives of treatment, alternative approaches, if feasible, and the potential risks. When appropriate, this plan should be submitted as a proposal to the owner, custodian, or authorized agent.

27. **Documentation of Treatment:** During treatment, the conservation professional should maintain dated documentation that includes a record or description of techniques or procedures involved, materials used and their composition, the nature and extent of all alterations, and any additional information revealed or otherwise ascertained. A report prepared from these records should summarize this information and provide, as necessary, recommendations for subsequent care.

28. **Preservation of Documentation:** Documentation is an invaluable part of the history of cultural property and should be produced and maintained in as permanent a manner as practicable. Copies of reports of examination and treatment must be given to the owner, custodian, or authorized agent, who should be advised of the importance of maintaining these materials with the cultural property. Documentation is also an

important part of the profession's body of knowledge. The conservation professional should strive to preserve these records and give other professionals appropriate access to them, when access does not contravene agreements regarding confidentiality.

EMERGENCY SITUATIONS

29. **Emergency Situations:** Emergency situations can pose serious risks of damage to or loss of cultural property that may warrant immediate intervention on the part of the conservation professional. In an emergency that threatens cultural property, the conservation professional should take all reasonable action to preserve the cultural property, recognizing that strict adherence to the *Guidelines for Practice* may not be possible.

AMENDMENTS

Amendments: Proposed amendments to the *Code of Ethics and Guidelines for Practice* must be initiated by petition to the AIC Board of Directors from at least five members who are Fellows or Professional Associates of AIC. The board will direct the appropriate committee to prepare the amendments for vote in accordance with procedures described in Section VII of the Bylaws. Acceptance of amendments or changes must be affirmed by at least two-thirds of all AIC Fellows and Professional Associates voting.

COMMENTARIES

Commentaries are prepared or amended by specialty groups, task forces, and appropriate committees of AIC. A review process shall be undergone before final approval by the AIC Board of Directors.

*Revised August 1994

Reprinted with permission of the American Institute of Conservation. A short link to the code of ethics is: https://www.culturalheritage.org/code.

This appendix is a reprint of the longer version (use the pdf link at the end of the shortened version) or go to: https://www.culturalheritage.org/docs/default -source/administration/governance/code-of-ethics-and-guidelines-for-practice .pdf?sfvrsn=21.

APPENDIX VII

"THE ETHICS OF DEACCESSIONING"*

STEVEN MILLER

With more than forty-five years in the museum field as a curator, director, consultant, museum studies educator, writer, and trustee, I have noticed that, in spite of a professed concern for the preservation of their collections, and in spite of the shock expressed when collections are lost to disastrous human or natural actions, museums are more than willing to engage in purposeful destruction of their collections.

Museums consciously trash things expected to be held in perpetuity for the public good by deaccessioning items without requiring preservation caveats of the next owner. This largely happens when museums sell items on the open market. To be sure, the vast majority of museum collections are secure for the moment. But as more and more institutions are overwhelmed by their expanding collections, and the cost of maintaining those collections, museum holdings will contract.

I have been fortunate enough that collection loss by outside forces in the museums where I have been a curator or director has not occurred (with the exception of a very large ship model on loan to another museum years ago). Yet I have caused depletion by my own overt and approved actions on the job when I have deaccessioned things commercially on the open market without restrictions.

Normally museums devote considerable resources to protecting their art, historic artifacts, and scientific specimens. Tens of thousands are employed in various museum jobs to help assure the retention of collections. These positions include curators, conservators, directors, collection managers, security, and maintenance staff. Though it appears museums are places for public engagement, enjoyment, education, and even entertainment they are really safe-deposit boxes writ large and made accessible to the public. The mission of most museums is to acquire and preserve valued evidence of the human and natural universe for the long term. Since forever is hard to assure with any certainty, "in perpetuity" is the accepted phrase applied on the job.

Except for loss of life, the most alarming tragedy that a museum fears is the destruction of its collections. Those in positions of authority recoil at the thought of objects disappearing from these cherished stores of our shared culture. Think of the theft of thirteen pieces of art from the Isabella Stewart Gardner Museum in Boston in 1990, the looting of the Iraq Museum in Baghdad in 2003, and the ransacking of the Mosul Museum by ISIS in 2015—all events that continue to reverberate today.

With strict security measures on all fronts and at all levels, museums work ceaselessly to guarantee the safe handling, retention, and exhibition of their collections. This devotion applies when items are in storage, in galleries, on loan, or in transit. Only employees trained to touch collections are allowed to do so. They will use certain kinds of gloves along with containers, wrappings, and equipment designed to come in contact with objects in a secure way. The spaces within which items are contained will be controlled to minimize pollution, light, or physical and chemical atmospheric harm.

When not being physically handled, museum collections are under the watchful observance of dedicated security systems and assigned personnel. Objects are protected by a host of safety measures, both technological and physical. When an item is on display, the first line of defense is the ubiquitous "Please do not touch" sign. These are, of course, simple reminders for well-behaved visitors. Augmenting written warnings are locked display cases, unbreakable glazed barriers, low and indirect lighting for light-sensitive items, alarms, stanchions, climate-control systems, and guards. Rooms and buildings that contain collections are basically vaults fitted out with locks, sprinkler systems, optical and sound security equipment, and devices to reduce theft and natural trauma. Updates based on new security information lead to regular improvements and museums spend serious dollars ensuring their systems are state-of-the-art.

The discipline of conserving art and artifacts, which combines science with manual training, is far ahead of where it was even a few decades ago. Its impressive progress is unfolding in exciting ways. But the many protections that conservation affords may be for naught when items are deaccessioned. While preserving items for sale is left unmentioned in a museum's mission statement, the sale of objects is commonplace. As practiced in the United States, unless there are ownership restrictions on objects, getting rid of unwanted collections is entirely legal. Moreover, it is accepted by all American museum profession membership organizations, such as the American Alliance of Museums and the American Association for State and Local History. There are scant warnings about how the practice may contradict museum ethics regarding the survival of objects entrusted to their care.

In the United States, most museums are privately owned and operated charities. They are classified as 501(c)(3) tax-exempt entities, governed by boards of trustees on behalf of the general populace. The boards do not own the museums or their contents; trustees are volunteers. Most have no museum experience whatsoever. Optimally, they rely on professional staff to run the institutions they oversee. But trustees have the final authority for just about everything a museum does, including both how it manages its collections and how it decides to remove objects.

Though it is largely accepted within the profession, deaccessioning is still a controversial issue. The debate surrounding it surfaces with alarming frequency. For the most part, however, complaints are rarely directed at the practice itself, but at what happens if any profits realized from the sale of museum collections are "misused." Furor tends to erupt only when income will cover operating expenses or capital and debt payments, rather than pay for future acquisitions.

Oddly, controversy about commercial deaccessioning sidesteps the fact that, unless the purchase is made by another museum, objects will probably be lost to the public forever. How does this practice align with the preservation imperative museums repeatedly embrace in all their actions and indeed by their very definition? Put simply: it does not.

Museum ethics is a popular issue these days. In regard to collections, the discussion tends to focus on the illegitimate ownership of things stolen from Jews by the Nazis that have found their way into museums, or objects in museums that were illicitly taken from countries once colonized by European nations. Rarely is destruction by deaccessioning a topic for debate.

Try and find out what happened to the items sold at auctions at Christie's or Sotheby's after the hammer comes down. Ask the selling museums and chances are slim they will be able to tell you where the items are now. Auction houses do not divulge buyers. This is understandable from their business perspective. I certainly have no idea where the few pieces that I and the boards to which I reported sold at auction years ago ended up. We might as well have tossed them on a bonfire. This is a total abrogation of museological duty.

What is the answer to this sort of deaccessioning destruction? How can it be avoided in an ethical manner? First: recognize this practice for what it is and acknowledge that it contradicts a museum's commitment to preserving and its ethic of caring for its collections. Second: rectify the practice. Third: hold participants accountable when their actions of deaccession violate mandates of caring for their collections.

Correcting the unfortunate results of unbridled commercial deaccessioning is simple. An item can be deaccessioned and kept by the museum for educational purposes. Or it can be sold or given to another museum. Everyone wins in this situation: The museum removing the item no longer has the expense of caring for it. The museum taking the object has expanded its holdings while agreeing to assure the item's future, or to transfer it again to another museum with the same donation restrictions. The public will still have access to it. And the object itself will survive, complete with its provenance.

The only absent players in this scenario are dealers of art and antiques, but they will be fine. Selling museum collections is a tiny part of their work. It should be noted that they are blameless when it comes to museum sales. They are simply doing their job for their financial benefit and for that of a client.

Inter-museum transfer of "unwanted" collections will be of immense importance ethically and practically to the museum field at large. It aligns with the preservation duty museums embrace, and it will end the obvious hypocrisy of voicing concern for the survival of collections, only to sell items into oblivion. Technological advances can easily facilitate a digital marketplace for museum–museum sales. One museum's loss can always be another's gain.

Inter-museum transfer need not rule out profit. A museum deaccession could happen commercially by sale only to other museums. This was done with a piece of sculpture years ago when I directed the Bennington Museum. A distinguished private dealer engineered the work's sale to a museum.

When I started my museum career, as a fledgling curator at the Museum of the City of New York in 1971, I never had a donor express concern that the museum would consider removing anything from its permanent collections. Now that deaccessioning is a common practice, the subject comes up often when discussing acquisitions and encouraging donors. I am always able to explain the relative rarity of the action, but I wonder what sort of donations museums are not offered because of deaccessioning fears. And of course, the vast majority of what you see in museums has been gifted.

Recently, I have tried to practice this type of ethical deaccessioning. In 2014, Boscobel House and Gardens in Garrison, New York, gave a mid-1850s painting of West Point to the West Point Museum, directly across the Hudson. Boscobel is a relocated, reconstructed, and conjecturally furnished Federal-period historic house museum from around 1810. The painting had absolutely no relevance whatsoever to the organization. The piece was officially deaccessioned by the Boscobel board of trustees at the recommendation of the board chair (Barnabas McHenry) and the executive director (me). These players hardly represented a big, famous institution. The painting is not by some high-profile renowned artist. Its commercial value is minimal. The West Point Museum at the United States Military Academy was delighted to receive it.

Large or small, notable or unknown, well-heeled or fiscally lean, just about every museum of any size, location, content, and governance structure could establish a policy to deaccession items only to other museums. Such a policy would accrue to the betterment of a collection object, the institution removing it, the receiving organization, the museum field, and those the field serves in general. It would be simple to accomplish by those who are responsible for the legacies held in trust for past, present, and future generations. It is also the ethical thing to do.

Note

*This article originally appeared in *The New Criterion,* 37, no. 4 (December 2018).

APPENDIX VIII

CORCORAN BOARD OF TRUSTEES ANNOUNCES ONE OF THE LARGEST FREE ART DISTRIBUTIONS IN U.S. HISTORY; MORE THAN 10,750 WORKS OF ART GOING TO 22 INSTITUTIONS IN WASHINGTON

—Multi-Year Process Evaluating Requests from Institutions Nationwide Leads to Distribution of 99 Percent of Corcoran's Art Collection to Museums, Universities, and Other Locations in the District—

WASHINGTON, DC—May 14, 2018—The Corcoran Art Gallery Board of Trustees today announced that more than 10,750 works remaining in the Corcoran's art collection will be distributed to 22 institutions across Washington in one of the largest free art distributions in U.S. history.

Today's announced distribution includes paintings, prints, drawings, sculpture, textiles, and photographs featuring internationally recognized artists such as Ansel Adams, Gene Davis, Walker Evans, Helen Franken-thaler, Sam Gilliam, Dorothea Lange, and many others.

Honoring the Board's previously stated commitment to preserve the Corcoran legacy in Washington, 99.4 percent of the Corcoran's total art collection will remain in the city. This includes today's distribution and 8,631 artworks previously accessioned by the National Gallery of Art after the Corcoran museum closed in 2014.

A complete listing of artwork and recipient organizations can be found on the Corcoran website at corcoran.org/artdistribution.

"I applaud the Corcoran Board of Trustees, who worked so diligently to honor the legacy of William Wilson Corcoran and keep the Corcoran's art collection in Washington. Residents, students, teachers, historians, and visitors from around the world will all benefit from these artworks being kept in DC, where they will be preserved and made available for the public to enjoy," said Washington mayor Muriel Bowser.

Recipient organizations include local universities (American University, The George Washington University, Georgetown University, Howard University, and the University of the District of Columbia); museums (Anacostia Community Museum, the National Portrait Gallery and seven other Smithsonian Institutions, The Kreeger Museum, the National Museum of Women in the Arts, the Phillips Collection, and the National Gallery of Art); and locations appropriate for specific artworks, such as the Supreme Court of the United States receiving a painting of Chief Justice John Marshall.

The recipient organizations will take possession of their selected artworks in the next few months, and they only pay for packing, transportation, and insurance costs. Additionally, the recipients have committed to keeping the artwork in the city for display and for student and scholarly study.

As is common with museums, approximately 80 percent of the art in the Corcoran collection is on paper, including drawings, prints, and photographs. Many of these are unframed and safely stored until needed for an exhibition or study. The bulk of the Corcoran's famous works on paper collection will be transferred to the American University Museum at the Katzen Arts Center where it will be preserved nearly in its entirety.

"As a proud member of the Washington Color School, I have a long history of creating and exhibiting my art in this town, and strong emotional ties to the city and its many cultural institutions. I am deeply gratified that the Corcoran's extensive art collection, from the Color School and so many other talented artists, will remain here in DC," said famed artist Sam Gilliam.

Of the entire Corcoran collection of 19,493 artworks, only 109 (0.6 percent of the total) are estimated to be leaving the District, including lace and other decorative work slated for the Smithsonian's Cooper Hewitt Design Museum in Manhattan, and 17 artworks going to locations having a specific connection to the work, the artist, and the Corcoran.

Distribution decisions were made by the Corcoran Board of Trustees after a multi-year process of evaluating requests submitted by institutions and organizations in Washington and nationwide. Three former Corcoran curators were hired to help evaluate these requests, and the curators operated under anonymity, so they could give candid assessments and recommendations to the Board.

"We are extremely pleased to distribute the Corcoran collection to so many worthy institutions across the city," said Corcoran Board of Trustees Chairman Harry Hopper. "The Corcoran legacy is threefold: The school, which continues operation as part of The George Washington University, educating future generations of artists; the building, which is getting the much-needed repairs and renovation to preserve it for the future; and the Corcoran art collection, which remains in Washington to be exhibited across the city for generations to come."

BIBLIOGRAPHY

Over the past decade several excellent books about museum ethics have been published. The subject is now included in relevant museum studies volumes of a more general nature. The topic will continue to attract authors. Be watchful for future writings.

Museum Ethics Publications

Edson, Gary. *Museum Ethics*. London and New York: Routledge, 1997.

———. *Museum Ethics in Practice*. London and New York: Routledge, 2017.

King, Elaine A., and Gail Levin, eds. *Ethics and the Visual Arts*. New York: Allworth Press, 2006.

Marstine, Janet, ed. *The Routledge Companion to Museum Ethics*. London and New York: Routledge, 2011.

Yerkovich, Sally. *A Practical Guide to Museum Ethics*. Lanham, MD: Rowman & Littlefield, 2016.

Museum Studies Publications with Germane References to Museum Ethics

Alexander, Edward P., Mary Alexander, and Juilee Decker. *Museums in Motion: An Introduction to the History and Functions of Museums*, 3rd ed. Lanham, MD: Rowman & Littlefield, 2017.

Ambrose, Timothy, and Crispin Paine. *Museum Basics*, 3rd ed. London and New York: Routledge, 2006.

Anderson, Gail, ed. *Reinventing the Museum: The Evolving Conversation on the Paradigm Shift*, 2nd ed. Lanham, MD, New York, Toronto, and Oxford: AltaMira Press, 2012.

Glaser, Jane R. *Museums: A Place to Work: Planning Museum Careers*. With Artemis A. Zenetou. New York and London: Routledge, 1996.

Courtney, Julia, ed. *Is It Okay to Sell the Monet?* Lanham, MD: Rowman & Littlefield, 2018.

Genoways, Hugh H., and Lynne M. Ireland. *Museum Administration 2.0.*, 2nd ed. Revised by Cinnamon Catlin-Legutko. Lanham, MD: Rowman & Littlefield, 2017.

Hein, Hilde S. *The Museum in Transition: A Philosophical Perspective*. Washington and London: Smithsonian Institution Press, 2000.

Jandl, Stefanie S., and Mark S. Gold. *A Handbook for Academic Museums: Exhibitions and Education*. Edinburgh: MuseumsEtc., 2012.

Kuruvilla, Heather Hope. *A Legal Dictionary for Museum Professionals*. Lanham, MD: Rowman & Littlefield, 2016.

Macdonald, Sharon, ed. *A Companion to Museum Studies*. United Kingdom: Wiley-Blackwell, 2011.

Malaro, Marie C., and Ildiko Pogany DeAngelis. *A Legal Primer on Managing Museum Collections*. Washington, DC: Smithsonian Books, 2012.

Miller, Steven. *The Anatomy of a Museum: An Insider's Text*. Oxford, England: Wiley, 2018.

Simmons, John E. *Things Great and Small: Collection Management Policies*. Washington, DC: American Association of Museums, 2006.

Online Resource

Institute of Museum Ethics, Seton Hall University MA Program in Museum Professions, South Orange, NJ, http://www.museumethics.org. This is an online site presenting and discussing museum ethics issues. It has a confidential inquiry component for anyone to submit questions about matters relating to museum ethics.

INDEX

Page references for figures are italicized.

ABOUT THE AUTHOR

Steven Miller has been working in the museum field for nearly fifty years. During that time, he has served as a trustee, director, administrator, curator, consultant, writer, educator, and lecturer, as well as media commentator on various topics relating to museum philosophy and operations. He is affiliated with the Museum Accreditation Program of the American Alliance of Museums. For sixteen years he was an adjunct professor, teaching several courses with the Seton Hall University MA Program in Museum Professions. He is the author of three books: *The Anatomy of a Museum: An Insider's Text* (2017); *Deaccessioning Today* (Rowman & Littlefield, 2018); and *How to Get A Museum Job* (Rowman & Littlefield, 2019). He holds a BA in sculpture (Honors) from Bard College and an International Graduate Certificate from the International Centre for the Study of the Preservation and Restoration of Cultural Property, Rome, Italy.